The Fearless Footballer

The Fearless Footballer

Playing without Hesitation

A Practical Guide for Building Everlasting
Self-Confidence in Football and in
Your Personal Life

By
Eitan Azaria

ISBN-13: 978-1517034023
ISBN-10: 1517034027

First printed in Israel on 2014
Translated by Helene Hart
www.onehourtranslation.com
Contact information: eitan@eitanazaria.com
www.thementalist.co.il

This book is dedicated with love to my dear parents Sima and Yaakov Azaria who taught me to stay true to myself in the toughest moments of my career.

Table of Contents

Foreword by Avram Grant

When I first met Eitan, he was still a young 18-year-old football player. Back then, I was the coach of the Israeli champions, Maccabi Haifa, and Eitan was playing for the club's youth team.

It took Eitan only one game to make an impression on me, and I asked him to join the senior team practice sessions.

Aside from Eitan's talent, passion and determination, he had one trait that stood out above all – the mental strength that characterized his game and that determinedly paved his way to the team's lineup the following year.

Eitan continued with Maccabi Haifa and managed to win two championships with the team, while I was appointed coach of the Israel national team.

Years later, our paths crossed again. This time was when Eitan had already become a recognized and well-known mental coach in Israel, and it was clear to us both that we would do something together. We founded *Win Your Mind* to help football players around the world fulfill their potential.

Whichever team I was coaching, be it Chelsea, Partizan Belgrade, Portsmouth or the Ghana national team, I always held the belief that success in football (and in life in general) is comprised of three parameters: talent, passion and mental strength.

The book that you are holding will teach you to develop the third and most critical parameter for your success — your mental strength.

I have always been impressed by Eitan's motivation, knowledge, will to learn, and willingness to share his knowledge. I am sure that this book, which contains proven tools and techniques to improve performance, will be useful to you. It is a must for any footballer aspiring to realize their inherent and full potential.

Good luck,

Avram Grant

Introduction and a Personal Message from Me to You

Hi,

I would like to congratulate you on purchasing this book, The Fearless Footballer — Playing Without Hesitation.

You have just joined a unique training program that will bring you immediate improvement in the personal ability, courage and confidence you demonstrate with every move you make, and in the pleasure you experience from the game that you aspire to be the best at.

Something very important before we begin:

This is not your standard book — this is a practical guide for creating change and true improvement in your career.

As such, if you plan on reading it without implementing the (very simple) tasks that you are about to receive, then I suggest that you ask for a full refund now.

Why?

Because a successful career consists of two compo-nents: fast learning + implementation…and you will learn plenty from this book — and fast!

However, if you do not apply the tools and methods I am giving you here, you will miss the most important stage in our process — the stage of seeing results on the field!

I know that you are here to see results in your career. I also know that you are putting your time, energy, hopes, desires and trust into getting ahead and making your dream career a reality.

I also know that you do not want to be on the field, hesitating before every pass, being concerned with what others think of you and then discovering at the end of your career that all your hard work was just a waste of time.

You are here to succeed! That is one thing I know for sure — and the simple fact that you are reading this book right now already makes you a more successful football player than 97% of all football players, who will never be free of the fears and concerns that sabotage the way that they play, game after game.

That is exactly what this guide is intended for — to enable you to build up your courage, your belief in yourself and your confidence, step-by-step, leading you to develop the personal ability that you need to become a prominent player in the competitive football world we live in.

N.B.: This book is not for weak players — it is a book for winners who want to be even more successful.

So if you are sitting down now, sit up!

Open up your chest and take the breath of a player who has confidence and pride…

Yes, yes, now! Don't think I don't see you.

Open up your chest, straighten your shoulders, hold your head up high, like the proud player that you are, take a deep breath, just the way the successful footballer that you aspire to be does.

That's right…and be proud of yourself for investing this time in yourself because we are going to have a great time together. You are going to go onto the field like a lion, already in your next game.

Warning

Although this book deals with developing your confidence and personal ability in football, you can expect to find that within 30 days your self-confidence will increase in other areas of life too: friends, romance, family, studies, work…and mainly — in 30 days' time — you will feel much calmer and happier, you will appreciate yourself more, and love being "simply you" in a way that you never imagined possible.

As such, when you read and implement this simple guide, you are going to say goodbye to the fears, concerns and worries that you may have had until now. You will get to know new friends called "fearlessness" "enjoyment" and "enhanced personal ability"!

Not only that. To give you the coaching message and mental tools in the easiest way possible, I have chosen to write this book as if I were talking directly to you, on the level.

So come on, let's get going.

Chapter 1

How to Use This Book to Eliminate Your Fears and Build up Your Everlasting Self-Confidence

So, what program are you going to experience with this book and how can you get the most out of it, so that you can play without inhibition and realize all that potential that you already have right there in your feet?

Well, that is really simple.

This book is divided into two parts:

Part One includes Chapters 1–4, in which you will learn the principles and benefits of fear and how to use them (you will need to read these chapters only once to understand the basic principles your improved personality and character will be built on. If you want to, you are welcome, of course, to read these chapters more than once).

Part Two includes Chapters 5–12. In these chapters you will learn simple techniques and methods for increasing your self confidence and coping with your most common fears. You will be able to implement what you learn in these chapters already in your next practice sessions, drills and games.

At the end of the book there is a personal letter waiting for you to read: "Successful Internal Dialogue — the Prayer for Winning." This letter is a personal prayer for you to read for 30 days, starting from the moment you finish reading this book (in the morning or in the evening before you go to sleep). This prayer will allow you to approach each game with peak confidence and a head free of concerns.

Warning: If you read this prayer without reading the book, the change you feel will not be significant. Trust me…I tested this on myself when I was younger, and it didn't work.

Why?

Because the most powerful learning and changes occurs after you understand…when you suddenly find yourself saying to yourself things like, "Ohhhhhhh….how did I not think of that before," or "I don't believe that I didn't know that before today,"…"How could I have played football without realizing that???!!!"

These are the moments in which you understand that you have started putting your new tools to work because real change in any field of our lives occurs when we begin to feel differently about things.

My goal here is to help you feel comfortable with yourself during every minute of the game, and by the time you finish this book you are going to enjoy playing in matches just as much as you enjoy playing with your buddies from down the road. You will enjoy taking risks, be hungry for the ball and full of confidence in the 90th minute so that you can win the game. You will find too, that during the entire 90-minute game, no disturbing thought such as "I wonder what other people think of me" will enter your mind and faze you.

The way to do this is to put your heart and soul into this book and to relate to it just as you do to your team's most important training sessions.

That is exactly what I did at nineteen, when I first started to work on my mind, and my career simply took off as a result. I won five titles in six years, two Cups as part of Maccabi Haifa's lineup in my first season, the Israeli State Cup, the Israeli Toto Cup, I went up a league…and yes — I dropped a league once too. I coped with tough lineup battles; I didn't always play full seasons. When I was with Maccabi Haifa FC I had to deal with really bad press that never gave me a break, but none of that stopped me from moving towards my goal — because success in football is not made up of successes only, but of your ability to pick yourself up quickly after the crises and pressure that your career bring you too!

So now is the time for you to decide.

Are you coming down this road with me or are you staying where you are?

You said that you are joining me, right?!...I'm really happy! Excellent.

So let's begin with a question.

What makes footballers begin a game with a sore stomach, heavy legs, a dry mouth, and a racing pulse that makes you panic during the game?

What makes players avoid the ball and hide the real football skills that are right there in their feet?

What is that thing that makes footballers play without confidence, hesitate before passing, avoid the ball, not take risks, and not try to score a goal even though the area is completely free?

So, if you are like me, I'm sure that you know the answer.

We both know that the first barrier to our real ability on the field is — fear!

Now, I know…I'm sure that you want to ask me, "Eitan, why the heck are you talking to me about feeling fear when all I want to do for myself is create success and confidence in my career?"

Well, the first reason that I want to talk to you about fear and how to overcome it in your career is that if you are going to spend most of your life feeling fear, tension, concern and pressure (in and out of the game), you will find it almost impossible to achieve the type of success in your career that you are aiming for.

In other words, if you allow mistakes, losses and turnovers to spark your fears — or worse, if you allow bad memories of games in which you demonstrated poor ability, the disregard of your coach, aggressive opponents, being benched, lineup battles to stress you out, you can expect to find yourself living a very frustrating and miserable life filled with constant stress and concern, which is what finally leads players to have the career of average and below-average players. That is not what we want to happen to us.

On the other hand — if you want to build a remarkable career (never mind how tough the competition around you is), if you want to be better on the field than your competition is at any given time, if you want to reach a point where no opponent, no spectators, no game and no important title will stress you out and get your feet confused right at the most critical moment of the game — then some part of you needs to learn to deal with that emotion called fear.

In order to achieve great things as a footballer, you need to be prepared to overcome fear

To help you get you into the first chapter of this book, I will quote two international star athletes, who are actually not from the football world (and you will immediately understand why):

The first quote is by Wayne Gretzky, the most famous hockey star in the world who said,

"You miss 100% of the shots you don't take".

The second quote is by the legendary basketball player, Michael Jordan, who said,

"I've missed more than 9,000 shots in my career. I've lost almost 300 games. Twenty-six times, I've been trusted to take the game winning shot and missed. I've failed over and over and over again in my life. And that is why I succeed".

I think that these important quotes and phrases can be used to turn us into successful footballers, because clearly these two athletes were at the top of their professional world.

Wayne Gretzky and Michael Jordan are considered to be the best athletes in the world in their respective fields, to this day.

Why?

Why them and not others?

Because as it turns out they understood something that most athletes do not …(and probably will not ever understand), and that is that in order to create career success, to achieve something great as a football player, you need to be prepared to overcome fear.

I want to share a small secret, just between the two of us…

Footballers are also afraid; the only difference between successful footballers and those who did not get far is that successful footballers do not stop in the face of fear!

13

They break through it, they destroy it, they do not allow any obstacle to stop them — and that is exactly what you too will be able to do when you use the techniques and approach that you will learn here right now.

Therefore, I would really like you to pay attention to every detail in this book, so that you can make significant leaps and bounds in your personal ability.

I'm sure that you feel good from the simple fact of knowing that fear is a natural part of our lives (and even more so in the lives of great athletes) — and that is OK.

We basically want to get to know our fear a little better so that we can control it — instead of it controlling us.

So, the first thing that we want to tell ourselves today is one of the following sentences:

"Today is the day I've decided to overcome fear and to show the true talent that is within me";

"Fear does not control me — I have full control over my life";

"I can learn to play freely, without hesitation".

Chapter 2

What Exactly Is the Fear That You Feel

So, we're on our way.

The first thing that will allow you to overcome fear and to realize your inherent potential is — to firstly understand what fear really is.

Well, fear is a paralyzing emotion caused by the thought that something dangerous is about to happen to us.

In other words, fear is the type of feeling that washes over us when we feel threatened and it awakens a sense in us that something dangerous is about to happen to us (something that could end in failure or disaster).

When does fear rear its head in football?

In football, we feel fear when we are about to make a pass but we are not sure that the ball will go where we intended.

When we are concerned that the final play we are planning won't succeed and that our teammates may then label us unreliable (and prefer to lose the ball than to pass to us).

Fear appears in us when on the one hand we want to get behind a player — but on the other we are concerned that that player will steal the ball from us and counterattack, which could result in a goal against us.

Fear awakens in us when we want to steal the ball — and we stop an instant before contact with the opponent because we're afraid of injury.

We feel fear when we arrive at an important game, or at try-outs for a new team, even though on the one hand we want to show our talent — and on the other, we are afraid to make mistakes and to hear the coach declare, "You aren't what this team is looking for — you're out."

When you are in a state of fear, you become someone else; I don't mean that you become someone horrible, I mean that as soon as that negative (and unpleasant) feeling overwhelms you, the feelings that immediately arise are anger, frustration, bitterness, irritation, tension and insecurity.

And those are the precise moments in which our decision-making process changes, which often leads to poor decisions We do not take risks, we do not dare, and we do not try to do those things that we do so easily at practice.

Fear also creates physical changes in us. In other words, fear has an immediate impact on the physical condition of our muscles, our legs become heavy, our hearts begin to race and we stop thinking clearly.

We hesitate before every pass, we avoid the ball, we don't take responsibility, we tentatively enter a tackle (or we don't get into a tackle at all).

I remember my first international game wearing the Maccabi Haifa uniform in the UEFA Cup playoffs. We played against Valencia in Rotterdam. I was nineteen and a half and I was sitting in the locker room. Although I was extremely well prepared physically, emotionally I felt something overwhelm me, a kind of apprehension and stress over what would happen. Suddenly, I felt my legs turn into lead, my heart began to race, and I found myself thinking, "What will happen if I can't handle their speed?"..."Just don't make any mistakes"..."The entire country and half of Spain will be watching this game — just don't do anything embarrassing."

In this book, you are going to receive the very same methods and tools that I used to overcome the terrible stress that could have ruined that entire game for me.

Clearly, if I had not known how to overcome the fear and stress that overcame me there, I would have very quickly lost myself on the field because when fear takes over we turn into players who avoid the ball. When we are overwhelmed with fear we play only to avoid losing (instead of to win).

Yes…I know that you are dying to be given ways to cope with your concerns and fears, and you'll get them soon enough. Trust me; I am no less eager than you are…

So what have we learned so far?

We have realized that fear is just a feeling that is created when we think that something dangerous is about to happen. If we change that feeling, we change our whole way of playing.

So then…how do we change the way we feel?

How can we bring ourselves to play and to make every move fearlessly and with high confidence that our play is going to succeed?

To understand how we can change how we feel, we need to understand that there are two types of fear. And that is exactly what you're going to learn in the next chapter, because that is where the gold is (and the trap that most players fall into).

Come on, come with me. I'm waiting for you.

Chapter 3

What Is True Fear and Why Are 97% of Your Fears on the Field Actually Fake?

Maybe nobody has ever told you this before, but it turns out that there are two types of fear — true fear and fake fear:

1. True fear — that is when there is true danger to our lives.
2. Fake fear — that is when there is no real danger to our lives, but we have possible scenarios running through our mind making our brain just as afraid as if our lives really were in danger.

We need to start differentiating between the two because that is our key to overcoming fear. So, let's talk a little about true fear.

True fear is when you need to cope with real danger and with a real threat to your life.

Here's a question for you — have you ever crossed a street when suddenly you hear the sound of a car or truck behind you?

What happened there, exactly?

Your eyes did not actually see the car behind you, and yet something made you instinctively dive for the sidewalk because you felt that if you didn't do something, something dangerous would happen to you (like for example, a truck would heaven forbid run you over).

But what made you sprint for the other side?

Why did things happen that way?

This is a good time to tell you about the brain's very special defense mechanism, which is so sensitive to danger that as soon as it detects anything that could be of any threat to you it does not ask you at all what to do, it simply takes over your body and makes sure that you move away from danger.

Much like a new mobile phone that arrives with a whole bunch of special apps and built-in features, we also come with a special mechanism in our brain — and that mechanism is really smart. It works exactly like a home alarm when we have a break-in.

What does the alarm at home do? It beeps and alerts you of danger, right?

Well that's exactly how your brain works!

You have a mechanism in your brain that physically prepares you for any imminent threat or danger, and that mechanism has one single purpose — to protect your life and make sure you don't get hurt.

Let's take another example:

Say that while you are reading this book, you suddenly see a roaring lion sprinting towards you, with bared teeth and a murderous look in his eye.

At that moment you don't say to yourself, "Hmmm…I wonder how many more sentences I can read before the lion gets here and devours me?"

Instead, what do you do?

What you do is run like crazy for your life so that you don't get eaten.

This reaction is called our "fight or flight" mechanism.

It is a mechanism with one aim — to help you cope with true fear (when there is true danger in your life), which is when there is true fear.

What is fake fear?

Fake fear is when there is no real danger to our lives, yet we make our brains think that our lives really are threatened.

I will repeat that again because that is the most important sentence in this book!

Fake fear is when there is no real danger to our lives, yet we make our brains think that our lives really are in danger.

We feel fake fear when we imagine all kinds of disastrous scenarios of failure in our minds.

Fake fear is when we focus on what we do not want to happen to us.

Fake fear is when we focus on turnovers, which we don't want happening to us, the coach yelling at us when we really don't want to be yelled at. It happens in that last bad pass that we don't want to give…and when that happens, we actually make our brains feel fear that is as powerful as true fear — as if our lives were really in danger.

In other words…

The problems that block our personal ability start when we turn fake fear into true fear in our minds.

I'll repeat that again (and I suggest you write this sentence down).

The problems that block our personal ability start when we turn fake fear into true fear in our minds

What do I mean?

I mean that in real life in the 21st century there is not much chance of real lions chasing after us to hunt us down, there are no trucks running us over right there on the field…but what we do have are imaginary lions and concerns that we create ourselves — even though in reality they simply do not happen.

Fake fear makes us focus on things that we do not want happening to us.

For example, a player that I worked with a year ago would reach a point that, if he lost two balls at the beginning of a game, the fear of making mistakes would overcome him and he would then play too tentatively.

Why?

Because the mere thought of losing more balls made him so tense he would become incapable of playing freely — he would simply play it safe and avoid the ball (instead of taking responsibility). He was also afraid that the coach would replace him if he lost another ball. When those types of concerns are running through your mind you cannot play as freely as you would expect of yourself.

It is true that fear is an inner feeling that footballers keep to themselves, but one can smell fear and see it in a person's body language. Fear is contagious and it makes others and your opponent take advantage of it when they smell it on you.

I remember back in my youth as a Maccabi Haifa player, I would see how the teams that were weaker than us on paper would come to our home field *Ketzef* for a game with fear in their eyes. It amazed me to see how fear could overcome a person before the game even started.

I remember that one of my aims as a right defender was to instill fear in my opponent, whether a midfielder or a center forward, and to make them feel threatened whenever they tried to get behind me.

My method was to close down my opponent right from the start, in every situation on the field. I would give him no room to breathe and would not allow him to receive a ball.

What amazed me was…sometimes I would be up against players who were taller than me by a head, and stronger than my physically…but the pressure we would put on them on the field would put them into a state of shock. I could see in their eyes that they were overcome with fear. I could feel how their fear mechanism would start taking over. Their body would prepare for a real threat to their lives — and in effect — all it is, is football. They were not under any real threat.

The thing is this…

When you interpret an event as a threat, your body reacts to that threat as if it was a real danger to your life.

What does this mean?

It means that your body cannot tell the difference between true fear and fake fear

If, as far as you're concerned, a lost ball is a critical mistake that to you is a sign that something bad is about to happen, then if you lose another ball, what your brain understands is that your life is in danger (even though all we're talking about here is football). When your brain feels a true threat to your life, it automatically prepares your body. Your muscles tense up, your breathing rate increases, your breath becomes more rapid, and your ability is impaired.

The biggest problem when that happens is that you get stressed out and tense up; you waste a lot of energy that you need to play the ball that you know so well.

What we need to realize is that the best players in the world are those who have failed countless times before they succeeded — and the secret to their success is that they "labeled" their failure differently...constructively. They interpreted and related to their failure in the completely opposite way from how other players often do.

Imagine if Messi, at fifteen, had stopped trying to get behind players because in some games they would steal the ball from him. Would he have made it to where he is today? Clearly not.

What would happen if Xavi or Götze stopped asking for the ball and conducting the game after their not-so-great games? Would they have attained the level of control and of playing they have today? You know the answer to that. In order to succeed, to be number one at your position, you must be able to pick yourself up and make the very same play needed over and over again, even if you gave the ball away two minutes earlier, or you missed scoring against the goalkeeper.

The real question is not if your fear is justified — it is if the fear serves you well and helps you to reach your goal

Why? Because when you worry constantly, all you're doing is practicing being worried.

When you worry about reaching the highest level or not — are you freeing yourself of concern? No! All you're doing is practicing worry.

The same goes for anger. When you're angry often because you may not have shown your true abilities yet, or because no clubs value you or recognize your potential, will your anger make you a better player? No! Because when you're angry a lot of the time all you're doing is practicing being angry all the time.

Will a player who drops their head and blames the world each time they made a bad pass become better at making more accurate passes? No! You and I both know that a player who drops their head and blames the world after every pass that didn't go the way they wanted is simply a player practicing to be a world-class "blamer."

In other words...

What you do over and over again is what you get better at.

If you worry all day about what will happen if you fail in your career — will that bring you success? Not at all! You're simply practicing being worried, sad, frustrated and mentally uneasy with yourself.

As such, what we want to do is to stop practicing fear and apprehension and to start practicing fearlessness.

I'll say that again...

What we need to do from now on is to stop practicing fear and apprehension and to start practicing fearlessness!!!

Because what you do time and time again is what you become better at. It's what you don't do that you get weaker at.

Being afraid is a habit!

I'll repeat that.

Being afraid is a habit!

Feeling offended and hanging your head after making a mistake is a habit.

Being constantly concerned with what others think of you is a habit that we ourselves have created. How did we create this habit?

We have simply trained ourselves really well to think the same thing….over and over and over and over again.

The good news is this…if we said that fear is basically a habit, habits are something we can change.

That is…

Just like the fear of losing a ball is a habit — you can also get used to wanting to receive the ball at every opportunity.

Just like avoiding tackles is a habit…so you can get used to playing more aggressively and physically (even if you are not built all that well).

Being fearless is a habit.

Playing with confidence is a habit (it is not pure luck).

We are going to start doing so in the next chapter.

So what do we have so far?

We know that basically, fear is only a habit that we have created ourselves over the years. We have trained ourselves really well to think about everything that can go wrong for us instead of focusing on what can go right for us.

We all have our fears...the fear that our career will end before our dream becomes a reality; the fear of disappointing our parents, our friends, ourselves; the fear of receiving the ball and getting confused at the last moment; the fear of receiving negative feedback from the coach. Fear before a game leads to legs like lead and a dry mouth...and if I carry on with the list this book will be infinitely long.

But...!

And we have a big but here!

As it turns out, all our fears, as human beings in general and as footballers in particular, lead to two main fears. Yes, that is what you heard...there are ultimately two main fears that make us worry, concerned, and show much less skill during games than we show during practice.

The first fear is — the fear of not being good enough
The second fear is — the fear of not being liked and respected

Underlying all our concerns, anxiety and fears, there are our two greatest fears.

The first concern — that of not being good enough — says that maybe I simply do not have what it takes to reach the high standard that I aspire to. The second is a continuation of the first, and it basically says that "if I am not good enough then I won't be liked or respected and I will then feel worthless as a player and as a human being."

When these two concerns are on our minds, there is a potential difference between your real ability and your belief that you can get there.

What do I mean?

I mean that each time there is a difference between your ability during practice and the ability you show in a game, it doesn't mean that you have forgotten how to play. All it means is that you are not thinking the right thoughts. All it means is that your approach to the game needs to be slightly adjusted to narrow the gap of your belief in yourself.

When you close that gap you'll feel that you are good enough to play with confidence. You'll feel that you like and think highly of yourself without needing anything from other people (i.e., without waiting for feedback or a good word — you won't need it). You will then be so at peace with yourself…so happy with what you are — that at that actual moment all the fans, your coach, opponents, will see you demonstrate ability that they had never imagined before.

Is that the way you want to be?

Then come on, let's start working, and in the next chapter we'll work on developing the most important habit a winning player has.

In the following chapter you will begin to understand the most important principle that will help you identify the success that lies behind your every fear.

So let's carry on to the next chapter and prepare for the most important chapter in your life.

Chapter 4

There Are 50,000 Fans Watching – How Come One Player Gets Excited While Another Chokes?

We're moving up a level...are you ready?

Because in this chapter you are going to understand the main principle that will help you to develop the habit that winning players have — the habit of recognizing the success that lies behind every fear.

In this chapter, I am going to tell you about the opportunity that is hidden behind every one of your fears.

Should we start?

Let's go.

It turns out that behind every fear that you have there is success lying there waiting for you to simply come and conquer it.

In other words, the reason behind failure could just as easily be the reason behind success.

And when I say that the reason for failure could equally be the reason for success I mean that the opportunity for success is right there within every fear.

Let's take, for example, two players before a game at Camp Nou.

The two are sitting in the locker room at Camp Nou before the game.

Player A tells himself: "There are 50,000 people out there – just don't blow it."

Player B tells himself: "There are 50,000 people out there – how great is that! Now is the time for me to show them what I'm worth."

What happened here?

We have the same incident; the same game.

Both players are in the same situation, but being in this situation before the game has made them feel completely different from each other.

One player interpreted the situation as one of pressure.

The second player interpreted the situation with healthy excitement and as an opportunity.

Why did this happen?

Because Player A was seeing the possibility of failure and player B was seeing the possibility of success.

In other words: The likelihood of losing the ball is the same as the likelihood of passing for a goal. The likelihood of having the ball stolen from you is the same as the likelihood of making a move in a 1 vs 1 situation and leaving your defender behind. The coach who is capable of yelling at you for losing the ball is the same coach who will complement or praise you after a good assist.

The fans who may curse you are the same ones who will applaud you after a good move.

Do you get what's happening here?

The very same fans, who may yell at you if you miss, are the same fans carrying you on their shoulders when you win.

That kick that may miss the goal could be the one that tears the net.

The assist that you aren't sure will work is exactly the same as the pass that may end the game.

Hiding within every game or tryouts that you are afraid you will fail in is the appearance of your life that will get you that huge contract.

Behind every fear of injury, there is also the fearlessness that makes your opponent want to stay far away from you.

Are you starting to see where I'm going with these examples?

What I would really like you to understand here is that in order to do well you must first begin to focus on what you want instead of on what you're afraid of.

If you want to make a good final pass stop thinking about what will happen if you lose the ball and focus instead on where you want the ball to go.

If you want to play for a good club stop thinking about what will happen if you're released and begin to focus on how you're going to become part of that team's lineup.

If you're tense before a game, don't concentrate on your opponents and on their advantages — focus on yourself and on your skills instead.

If you want to steal the ball from your opponent then stop thinking about what will happen if they get behind you — and start focusing on the ball that you want to steal when you're going 1 vs 1.

Do you see how a tiny change in your way of thinking can make an enormous change in your ability?

Because in every situation you can choose between two ways of thinking:

1. Focus on what can work — or —
2. Focus on what can go wrong.

Every time you focus on what could go wrong and on what you're afraid of, you're basically fighting fear. On the other hand, whenever you focus on what you want to happen, your fear will see that you mean business — and at that moment it will have no choice but to go along with you and support you.

What is happening here, basically?

What is happening is that we, as people, have our own personal judge right there in our heads, and that judge is the one deciding what is good and what is bad. That judge is actually our own inner voice deciding for us what is dangerous and what is not.

By the way, your inner judge is not a bad person; just the opposite. However, because it cares about you, it also worries about you failing — and what that judgmental voice does to stop you from failing is warn you of the dangers.

That is why you feel pressure when you receive the ball. It is not because you have all of a sudden forgotten how to play football. It is your inner voice talking to you and saying things like, "What am I doing now?"..."Please don't let me lose the ball!"..."What will happen if I mess up and get yelled at?"

When those types of sentences constantly run through your head your brain doesn't notice that in exactly the same situations something good could happen, like an accurate pass, a smart ball. Maybe you'll retain the ball and enable your team to reposition?

So many good things could happen on the field at any given moment but when your head is constantly thinking only about what could go wrong, naturally your body and brain do not notice the next good move that you could be making.

As such, the first principle I would like to teach you is very simple:

Focus on every pass or move,

not on the failure you're afraid of

Great players think about how the next pass can work while all the others think, "What will happen if I mess up?"

Great players focus on the opportunity to score, while the others focus on their fear of missing.

Great players know that there will always be people with something to say and they play for themselves…and the others? They want to please everyone.

A successful goalkeeper focuses on taking the first ball. The others focus on hoping to avoid the ball.

Can you see this small difference between success and failure? Why does it happen? Because what you focus on is what grows!

If you focus on failure — your brain will make sure to find it. If you focus on success — your brain will do all it can to find success.

But this is the most important thing to understand!

If you focus on success will you be able to ensure success in your every move? Well, we both know that the answer is no. We are, after all, only human; and we cannot always be perfect (and by the way, Messi, Cristiano and Götze are not perfect).

But!!!!...an important "but":

If you focus only on failure, what will happen?

That's right.

You will make sure that you fail! You won't even have a small chance of succeeding.

So what have we learned?

We've learned that you have two options to choose from for your every move in the game:

1. To choose to focus on the success of that move;
2. To choose to focus on the possibility of that move failing.

What you choose to focus on has a direct impact on your personal ability.

Focusing on the first option will help you approach every move with confidence and fearlessness (because your brain will react "enthusiastically" to the idea that the move is likely to succeed). Focusing on the second option will make you play tentatively (because your brain will "fear" the implications of failure such as the coach yelling, being replaced, being benched).

Remember, great players ask themselves, "How am I going to make this move work here," while the others approach the move while telling themselves that "there is no way they can do this and the opposing team are going to steal the ball."

As such, your job for the next training session and game is really simple:

Start focusing on the success that your next move may bring — not on giving the ball away or on failure

Start focusing on the success that your next move may bring — not on the failure that can happen or on losing the ball

The best way to start practicing this is after a mistake, a stolen ball, the coach yelling and at any other time that it may be easier for you to feel disappointment and to hang your head.

Between us, when you perform a move well, it is easier to approach the next with confidence, faith and motivation.

When everything goes well for you in the game you don't need my help to look for your next success.

The trick is to look for your success after you've made mistakes, after lost balls, at moments of pressure during the game. These are the moments that turn you into a real "star" and leader that everyone follows.

As such, your mission from this day on is to relate to every move separately.

Great players understand that there is no connection between moves. Your aim is to always look for success in your next move. Even if you have made four plays that have ended in lost balls, you still need to be on the lookout for your next successful move.

Remember:
Losers replay their last mistake in their minds while winners run for the next success that is just around the corner

and you want to chase success from this day on!

To chase success you need to be prepared to recover fast from mistakes and crises that happen to you during the game.

Winners don't waste time between moves.

One move is over — boom! They are already on the lookout for the next play. They lost a ball? Boom! They return quickly to the game and put the pressure on. Other people are cursing them from the stands? Boom! They simply smile and carry on running, knowing that they are their own biggest fan.

Do you understand?

Your task is to reach the end of the game with more positive moves than negative. For that to happen, you need to create a lot of moves and to look for the best that could happen in all of them.

So — I've prepared a personal letter for you. I recommend that you read it before practice and games over the next week.

The letter goes like this:
Today, I choose to focus on the success I see for myself (and not on failure). I realize and accept

that to focus on success will not always promise me success in every move but if I focus on the failure that I fear I will have no chance of doing well.

From this day on I promise to approach each move while looking for the success it could bring — not the failure.

I know that true failure is not looking for success in every move.

I have already proven to myself, hundreds of times, that focusing on success enables me to identify more passing, kicking and stopping opportunities than if my head is occupied with possible mistakes.

I know that mistakes are part of the game and although they do not feel good I promise to pick myself up and look for success in the very next move. I know that when it happens to me, I will go back home filled with pride in myself for not giving up on myself.

Chapter 5

From Zero to Hero: How to Use Arjen Robben's Secret Mental Weapon

I don't think there is any better example to demonstrate the power of "going after your next success" than that of Arjen Robben, a player for Bayern Munich, in the UEFA Champions League final.

Robben's story in that final is a classic story of achieving success after failure. As I am sure you remember Robben brought a bag of failures with him to that game from previous important games.

Robben lost in the FIFA World Cup in South Africa, which included his hair-raising missed goal against Iker Casilla — one that could have secured the match and sent the Netherlands home holding the cup. He had two losses in the two UEFA Champions League finals (in 2010 and in 2012, he missed a penalty shot in shootouts against Chelsea). He missed a penalty shot and a shot into an empty net in the final minutes of the seasonal game in Germany, during the 2011–12 season, when the score was 0:1 to Dortmund, leaving Bayern six points behind with only four rounds to the end of the season. That was enough to award the Bavarians the title of runners-up.

Robben himself said after the game, "That is very bitter and very disappointing. In the last three years I have converted 10 or 11 penalties in succession. That was the first one I have missed and, yes, that was really embarrassing."

All of Robben's failures were still fresh in the minds of all the fans that came to the 2013 finals.

The failures were not on Robben's mind at all

He had never been a coward

And if you saw that final then I'm sure you saw how he came to receive the ball time and time again after his biggest mistakes and worst misses (as if he had never made a mistake).

And by the way, Robben began that final on the wrong foot too. Already in the 30th minute he missed his first shot and everyone was certain that Robben was on his way to yet another miss in his career — but not Robben.

Robben carried on playing as if he had never failed because what everyone else saw as failure (misses and mistakes) Robben saw as learning and as an opportunity to improve before the next time.

It was evident in his body language that here was a person who tries constantly and who believes in himself (unlike other players who avoid playing when things go slightly off-track for them).

What was special about Robben over the years was that he could keep his cool during both failure and success. Robben knew that the game would go on, with or without him, and as a player who aspires to be the best he could not allow himself to waste time mourning every bad move.

Therefore, Robben didn't judge himself after unsuccessful moves either. He didn't get mad at himself; he didn't mess around and freeze on the spot. He simply took himself in hand and returned determined to his position — because only one thing interested him…looking for the next opportunity.

The game continued, as did Bayern's and Robben's lack of success and misses, but when failure is not an option for you, you don't stop until you reach your goal, and Robben's moments of glory arrived when he assisted on the first goal, scored the second, and carried Bayern to their fifth victory of the UEFA Cup.

And what were the headlines in the next day's papers?

That's right! Arjen Robben is a winner.

Only two days earlier, he was crowned the biggest loser in all of Europe...and suddenly, after 90 minutes he is crowned the king?

How did that happen?

It happened because of one principle that is important to your success and that you may know — if you don't, then now is the time to familiarize yourself with it now because it is critical to your success.

This principle is called the "We Knew You Would Make It" Principle

The "We Knew You Would Make It" Principle says that all those people who do not believe in you today will be the first to jump up and tell the world that they knew you would make it when you do.

I will never forget how, when I was 13 years old, the cab drivers would laugh at me whenever they drove me to Maccabi Haifa's youth team practices.

They would tease me constantly and tell me that I had no chance of making it, and that a kid from *Ma'alot* had no chance of going far. I will never forget how, when I was 20 (seven years later), three weeks after winning the State Cup with Hapoel Ramat Gan, after being signed by Maccabi Haifa for five years, I brought the cup home with me to *Ma'alot* (it is customary for each player to take the cup home for a day). Half the town came to my home to have their photo taken with the cup. My home became almost a shrine — and guess who were the first ones there to have their picture taken?

That's it! The cab drivers…

What is the first thing that they said? You're right again.

"We drove him to practice! We helped him make it and we supported him all the way," when in fact they did not support me at all (actually they didn't really give me much thought at all).

Why am I telling you this?

Because those people who may not believe in you today — will be the first to jump up to tell the world that they knew you'd make it big.

So, from this day on you're going to stop allowing people's reactions, criticism and remarks to influence your mood in any way. What others say is their opinion…their belief — and you do not have to agree with it.

If they tell you to "leave it, you can't make it in the team you're with," and you believe that, then what are the odds that you'll start the game confident that you are going to do well? You got it. Zero.

Take, for example, the Brazilian Marta Vieira da Silva who became the all-time top scorer of the Women's World Cup in 2015, with 15 goals.

Marta always knew what she wanted and never let anyone's opinion stop her. As a young girl growing up in a poor town in Brazil, she had to fight to get to play. The boys she played with on the streets often shunned her because they didn't like being outplayed by a girl. Her brother, who wanted to protect his younger sister, was also opposed to her playing.

She was later banned from playing with the boys.

Did she let this stop her?

Not at all. Her brother's opinion, the rejection, and the insults she received for playing football did nothing to hold her back.

Marta Vieira da Silva remained focused on her goal and true to herself, and she was discovered by the Brazilian coach Helena Pacheco when she was 14 years old. She moved to Rio de Janeiro to train with the Vasco da Gama women's club, which ceased operation only two years later. This too, did not stop her. She stuck to her goal, and became the first Brazilian woman to play professionally in Europe.

To list all of Marta's achievements we would need a whole chapter. To mention a few, she was named FIFA World Player of the Year five consecutive times, the Golden Ball at the 2004 FIFA U-19 Women's World Championship, and the Golden Boot award in the 2007 Women's World Cup.

Do you see where I'm going here?

I'm trying to make a very simple point, which is that you are your own best fan. You need to be able to encourage yourself more than anyone else over your entire career.

You won't always receive support and encouragement from others. Not because they are bad people in any way, but because they simply do not believe in themselves. And because they do not believe in themselves they will try to project their own lack of faith in themselves onto you, only to make themselves feel better. After all, we all know that everyone jumps at the chance of being with you when you succeed, don't we?

Why?

Because people like to be connected to success. They will do anything they can to feel a part of success, and they will do anything they can to avoid having anything to do with disappointment.

Everyone, especially those people who do not really believe in you right now, will be right there with you when you make it, they will all call you, want to hang out with you, interview you, and they'll tell others that you're friends.

Your aim is to go your own way. Even when you do not receive the full support of those around you, and mainly after failures...which leads me to the next principle, which says that you need to be your own best friend (because nobody will support you like you can support yourself).

You yourself should be the one to support you without waiting for anyone else to do so. Don't let other people's lack of faith in themselves turn into your own lack of faith in yourself.

And this leads me to reveal the well-guarded mental secret of successful footballers.

This is the secret that turned Robben into the winner of the UEFA Champions League in that well-known game against Dortmund.

The secret says the following:
The true recognition and respect one needs in life is the recognition and respect that you give to yourself

What does that mean?

It means that just like you'll have plenty of good moves, you will also make mistakes and lose balls. The coach, your teammates or the fans will not always support you and cheer you on after each mistake...why? Because the reactions of the coach, the players, the fans are not under your control.

There is, however, one thing that is under your control — and that is your own response to yourself. You are the one who can pick yourself up better than anyone else in the world!

Winners do not wait for the fans to cheer them on to play hard — they do it themselves because that is who they are.

Why am I telling you all this?

Because winners have something that others don't. Winners have a unique relationship with themselves!

Winners are those athletes who take care of the most important thing that they have — being their own best friends.

That is exactly what Arjen Robben did from the moment he stepped onto the field.

Just between you and me, Robben was very easy to dislike. He constantly made those around him feel like there wasn't a thing he couldn't handle, that nothing could break him. After giving the ball away he would return to the defense like a lion, his face calm and relaxed and his head raised high and proud, his shoulders back, running lightly.

On the face of it, it seems natural, but behind that body language there was clearly the thinking of a player who gives himself support during every single minute of the game. As such, your assignment for today is to start strengthening your personal relationship with yourself because if you don't give yourself support nobody will do it for you. Even if others do support you when you don't — it is worthless because you cannot control the support you receive from others — and it won't always be there.

If you do not support yourself and have your own back in every situation, you will quickly discover how far you are from fulfilling your potential (because if you do not support yourself and believe in yourself then the best team in the world will not be able to help you to be a leading player).

So…during the next 30 days (from the day you finish reading this book) you are going to become your own best friend (because nobody will give you support the way you can give yourself support).

The support you give yourself comes in two parts:

1. Support and encouragement during the game — after you make mistakes / lose the ball, and
2. Support and encouragement off the field — in the face of other people's negative opinions.

In the same way that good friends help each other in times of trouble, your aim is to support yourself through difficult times too.

How can you become your own best friend? There are three rules for what not to do and another three for what you should do (note that the "what not to do" rules at the moment are more important than the "what to do" rules are):

So, it goes like this…during a game there are three things that you must never do:

1. Do not judge yourself during a game!
2. Do not put yourself down!
3. Do not analyze any play that is over.

What should you do?

1. Encourage yourself and speak positively with yourself!
2. Raise your head and use the body language of a winner (like that of Robben)!
3. Look for your next play after making a mistake during the game!

Note: The three "what not to do" rules are much more important than the "what to do" rules are, because if you do not judge yourself or put yourself down during the game (using internal dialogue such as "You look like such a loser"…"You can never finish a game without messing up") you are going to feel better automatically, your body will feel that it can rely on you, and that will help you make your next play with confidence.

Someone who gets stuck after giving the ball away and who's head drops is a player who will not get very far professionally not because they lose the ball but because they recover slowly as a result.

Recovering slowly between moves is an indication of self-judgment, and we do not want to do that.

So, from this day on you are going to throw away all statements such as:

"You looked like such a loser!"

"You never finish a game without making a mistake!"

"You couldn't even give one good pass!"

Instead, you will start telling your body things like:

> "The best players also make mistakes, I'm moving on!"

> "I have no control over that mistake anymore, but I do have full control over my own reaction, I'm moving on!"

> "I trust myself!"

"I believe in my own ability!"

"I give myself permission to move forward!"

"Relax!! Don't stand still!"

"I have game!"

Your aim is to get to the end of each game while making sure that the total of all your positive plays is greater than the total of your negative plays.

Does that say that you won't make mistakes?

Clearly you will make mistakes. And that's OK, we want you to make mistakes because the only perfect players in our world are those who are always on the bench — they have never made mistakes, and you do not want to be there.

Chapter 6

Turning Fear into Your Best Friend – Is It Possible?

So how can we beat fear, I'm sure you're asking…

Well, this is the thing — we don't want to beat it, we want to make it our best friend so it'll stop driving us up the wall and hounding us (because good friends are people who take care of each other, and who want us to feel good).

That is exactly what you're going to do with your fear — you're going to turn it into your number one fan.

The truth is, each time you try to fight your fear, it will fight you right back. And we don't want that happening to you.

But what does "turning fear into your best friend" even mean?

When I say that we need to turn fear into our best friend, what I mean, just between you and me, is that fear is a coward and so we need to help it see the opportunities in each play we make on the field instead of allowing it to show us all the mistakes that could happen in each move.

And the only person who can help your fear gain confidence is you.

It isn't your fault that nobody has told you that the power to control your fears and concerns is in your own hands.

However — it is 100% your responsibility, from this day on, to make sure that you are the one in control of the fear, instead of it controlling you.

Fear can be controlled if you talk to it as if you were talking to your friend, and show it that there is another option; that as one person, you have a greater shot at succeeding if you focus together on success (instead of focusing on failure).

The fastest, coolest and most fun way to do this, which has worked for me whenever I have felt stressed out, worried or afraid in any way, is to talk to your fear; to explain to it that you are both here to succeed and that you need it to help you instead of trying to trip you up.

Yes, really talk to it as if it were your friend sitting right there in the room with you.

And now I want you to have this method so you too can befriend your fear, discover that it can be your best friend, and see it become one of your most enthusiastic supporters— one who will walk through fire and water with you.

If you read and implement the simple exercise I am going to give you right now, you can expect to feel an instant sense of relief, confidence, and incredible calm before the game (and in your career in general). I warn you, it is addictive!

So, what you're going to read now is a short letter that you will use to talk to your fear with, and when you read it, it is vital that you mean every single word that you say, and imagine that your fear (now a real pest) is simply sitting there and listening to every single word.

Imagine that your fear is like a person who really enjoys listening to everything you say, and pay attention to the change your fear goes through while you are reading. Notice how, while you are reading, your fear (that you may be feeling in your body) slowly disappears, and a sense of ease and confidence take over your body in its place.

So go on then, take a deep breath.

In your free time, invite your fear to have a short conversation, and note how that fear (soon to become confidence) is suddenly really happy to finally have your attention. It is even a little embarrassed. Sit facing each other, and begin:

Dear Fear,

Firstly I would like to thank you for being in my life. I know that you are here to warn me and stop me from taking risks because you are afraid that I will make mistakes during games. I also know that your intentions are good when you warn me that something dangerous might happen to me during a game.

However, dear Fear, when you warn me too often and tell me not to attack a player or to not even try to score or to give a smart pass, or to play a relaxed game the way I know I can, well maybe your way I really don't make mistakes, but I also don't fulfill my potential or stretch my limits.

So today I want to ask for your help. Today I want you to help me to improve and take risks on the field with confidence; to jump at a high ball with full belief that I will be the one to take the ball; to love to receive the ball — and to be someone who can lose it too.

After all, dear Fear, we are together here in this body, and I know that deep within you, you too want to be great at football and to become the best player possible, but it won't happen if you're always warning me of what could go wrong before any play I make, like a worried grandma might do...

So today I need your support and help in a joint effort to see the success that can come from any move I make, because only in that way can I approach the ball with confidence. That is the only way I can begin a game with a smile on my face. I know that we may not have talked about this before, and it's true that I've tried to ignore you and avoid you, and that is why you've chased after me without giving up on me — because you care about me and want what's best for me.

But today I don't want to avoid you anymore, and I know that you are fed up with running after me all the time, so today is the day that we become a team, and I'm happy that you're smiling now because that means that you have also been looking for me in order to give me the confidence and support that I need.

Now, I know that you'll let me begin each game feeling like there is someone who trusts me — and that is you...in the same way that you've kept me out of danger until now. I already feel that you have my back, and that you're going to trust me and support me in the way I need you to. And I am so happy we had this talk because having you with me on our way to fulfilling our shared dream helps me to relax. I also see clearly that with your help, together we will become an enhanced version of who I am now. I know that we can be good friends. I already feel that inside, and I already know because you have agreed to trust me and support my actions, that we are beginning an amazing journey together. We are going to go onto the field and show everyone that we're unstoppable on the field when we work as a team.

Love you, dear friend.

When you finish reading the letter, I want you to imagine fear as a person who comes over and gives you a great big warm and supportive hug.

When you do this wholeheartedly you discover that fear is a pretty nice and good person just like you are — you discover that fear is someone who only wants to help you, and this letter will help fear become a good friend, just like an older sibling who is there to support you in all that you do.

I suggest that you read this letter at least seven days in a row (and if you want to do a mental leap, read it in the evening, before you go to sleep, before each game).

You'll be surprised to discover just how fast your body will feel more relaxed. Your legs will be lighter than ever before. Your head will be free of thoughts, and your performance will improve to such an extent, you will not even remember ever feeling tense before a game.

That's it...we're done for this chapter. To be honest, I am really curious to hear how your talk with your fear (now your friend) went.

I know that it is not usually the done thing in a book, but I would please me greatly if you wrote and told me how this method worked for you. Here's my personal email address so now I too am your friend. I would truly like to hear how it worked for you, and how you felt after you spoke with your fear, now your best friend.

My personal email address is eitanaz2@gmail.com

Chapter 7

Fail More = Succeed More!

Yes, you read the name of this chapter right. It is "Fail More — and You'll Succeed More!"

What do I mean?

Many studies have been done on the theory of success in all fields of life: sport, business, relationships, parenting, and so on...and one of the best and most reliable ways to study the reasons for success was to find the most successful people in each field, to interview them and to find their common denominator and main reasons that they share and that make them experts in their field — so that other people could use the same modes of thought and action to reach similar results.

What does that have to do with you?

Take note! When this subject was first studied, elite athletes, famous TV stars, successful businesspeople, etc., were all asked what the number one reason for their success was, and almost all of them replied immediately with the following answer:

"We failed more times than others. That is the main reason for our success."

"What does that mean," they were asked. Most of them gave the same answer:

The fact that we failed more times than others does not mean that we failed. It means that we gained more experience than others in our fields, because in contrast with those who never dared to try and who quit after one failed attempt, we went back to that point of failure with our heads held high, pride in who we were, and curiosity. We tried to get past that point we'd failed at in the past, and we made quite a number of mistakes, but each time we failed we approached it from another angle, with a slightly altered program.

We tried to get beyond that point where we'd failed in the past, and we made quite a number of mistakes. But whenever we stumbled, we tried again from a different direction, with a slightly altered approach until in the end we had made many attempts, some of which worked and some of which didn't. Finally, when we did succeed, we understood. We understood what worked and what didn't. And here is where the fun bit begins because at that stage we didn't need to try anymore because we already knew what did and didn't work, and that was our real victory.

What have we learned here, basically?

That successful people do not have any super powers… they don't have wings, a magic wand or any special qualities that you don't have.

So what do they have?

People who have made it think and act differently from others.

When successful people run into a problem, they become enthusiastic and curious. When other people run into difficulty they simply quit ("because basically, who feels like trying to improve, give me a break").

And it's the same in football.

The best football players hunger for the ball and to be part of the action, even at the cost of giving the ball away, making mistakes, or receiving criticism.

Why are they like that?

Because they understand that the more involved they are in the game, the more experience they will gain, until the move that was once strange and new becomes automatic.

Failure is the most important stage on the way to success.

You need it more than you think. And I'll tell you more.

If you really want to make it big, you'll aim to fail as much as you can and as soon as you fail, you'll search quickly for the next attempt because when you fail often and quickly get back up again for your next play, you're actually teaching your brain to get into the pace of playing with the big timers.

The pace of big time games is a very unique one, and what makes it unique is that there are no pauses between moves. To put it simply, great players don't think between moves, they try something on the field and as soon as it's over they have already moved on to the next move — without analyzing, without brooding — they simply say the magic word: NEXT. They look for the success that is waiting for them in their next play.

The best football players understand that their greatest mistake would be to start thinking between plays on the field.

When great players lose a ball, they run like crazy and ask for the ball time and time again, while all the others lower their heads and blame themselves.

When successful football players receive harsh criticism from their coach or from spectators they take it well because they understand that they can show better ability, and that all they need to do is to find a way to improve.

All the other players start to avoid the ball after they receive criticism.

So when I say "the more you fail — the more you succeed" what I mean is that the moves that you don't make are doomed to fail 100% of the time.

What this means is that your aim is to strive to make as many moves as you possibly can.

But what will happen if you make mistakes? You'll do exactly what all successful football players do. What do they do?

They relate to and interpret their failure as a learning opportunity and use it as a step to improve, unlike others who interpret failure to be the end of the line for them.

As such, from this day on I suggest you adopt a new belief for your career, and that new belief is:

Every single one of my results on the field is an achievement — There are no failures; there is only feedback for progress!

"All my results on the field are achievements!
There is no failure - only feedback to learn from!"

What this means is that if you have taken action and made the play you believed to be right, you have already achieved. Yes, there are times when you succeed and times when you don't, but the beauty here is that it doesn't matter if you succeed or not. Your aim is to learn and to improve yourself in preparation for your next play.

On the one hand there is no way you can improve if you relate to every mistake as a disaster. On the other, you will definitely improve if you relate to every mistake as an opportunity to perform your next play well.

That is how great footballers work, and I know that you are going to work in exactly the same way because your success is the most important thing to you.

So, your aim from now on is to strive to execute the skills that you may have feared using until today because you now understand that your real fear should not be of the mistake — but of what will happen if you don't try.

"Not trying" is what you really need to fear, because the real truth is:

You have nothing to lose — you can only gain from each move you make.

I'll tell you more than that.

In order to become a leading first-team player who is the best in their position, you need to gain experience in every play a player in your position would ever need to make. In other words, in order to be an excellent defender you need to be number one at closing down a diagonal ball, man-to-man defense, taking a kick in motion, and positioning.

To be an outstanding midfielder you need to be great at escaping stressful situations and breaching the defense. You need to be accurate, aggressive and audacious (in the positive sense of the word, of course). How do you think experienced players built up their own confidence and gained experience? You're right — through failure.

In other words, they failed a great many times, and because they failed so often and moved on, at some stage they also developed a style that not only made them more stable as players, but it also gave them confidence that could not be undermined by their own mistakes; it turned them into fearless footballers.

To reach such high levels yourself, you need to award yourself this gift. If you strive to put yourself in as many situations possible that would once have scared you, and if you do the play you wanted to execute well, you will be happy.

However, if you did so happen to make a mistake…if you lost a ball…if you were yelled at by the coach — it doesn't matter. Remain calm, accept your mistake as a fact that cannot be changed and approach it from a slightly different angle.

For example:

A right midfielder will carry on trying endlessly to break through and to break through and to break through the defense and will not give up when nothing is working for them. At a certain stage the player will realize what was good and will carry on doing it, and will stop doing things that didn't work…but you won't know what does and what doesn't if you don't try.

If you want to become great at taking kicks, will two kicks a week after training be enough? Of course not.

You need to practice the plays you want to be the best at time and time again otherwise your body will not get used to it.

As such, your assignment for this chapter is very simple:

1. Choose the move that hasn't gone too well for you until now in a game; one that you know is part of your drills but that you haven't managed to perform well in a game yet.

   Your aim is to attempt that move as many times as you can in a game.

   Yes, even at the cost of not being able to do it well every time, because you need to fill your experience bank in order to see what works and what doesn't.

2. Later, when you go home, analyze and ask yourself what worked and what didn't. Don't judge yourself, don't put yourself down! That is not the purpose of this exercise. The purpose is to identify what worked and what didn't in your performance.

3. You'll see that the more you perform the same plays over and over and over again, the more comfortable you'll feel, and the other players will get used to the fact that it is part of your game. (These plays can include: a creative pass between two players; receiving the ball in the danger zone; making a smart move with the

ball; simple play; aggression.) That's how you'll build up your stability in those skills.

*Note that what is important here is to repeat the same plays time and time again; each time from a different direction until you find the right way to perform the plays you want to do well.

Chapter 8

Changing the Fear of Failure — into the Drive for Success!

In this chapter I am going to teach you a simple method, and if you implement it you will be able to overcome every fear, worry and source of pressure that you've had until now.

The method I'm going to teach you here is called "Turning Fear into Drive."

What we're going to learn here is how to turn fear, which is there to hold us back, into drive, which makes us want to do what we were too afraid to try until now. In other words, one of the fastest ways of coping with that paralyzing fear is to find a greater fear (I call that positive fear), which will make you eliminate your earlier fear. You will become driven and motivated, which will get your body moving and fearlessly performing the move that you have avoided doing until today.

So how do we turn fear into drive?

Let's start with an example.

Let's say that your biggest fear until now has been to make a critical mistake that will make all the other players yell at you and stop passing to you, and because of that fear you've been playing tentatively and safely. If that is the case, your greatest fear doesn't need to be "what if I make mistakes" but of carrying on playing safely and ending up with the career of an insignificant player that draws no attention — if anything that is what needs to scare (and motivate) you. If you play it safe and don't show what you're capable of then you'll never be an exceptional player and you will be invisible. Is that what you want? I know that it isn't.

So, then what do you prefer — to not make any mistakes and to end up with a mediocre career — or to make your mistakes and give yourself the opportunity to become a one-of-a-type player who nobody can forget?

Let's take another example:

If, until today, your greatest fear has been of injury, and that is why you don't get into tackles and don't play hard, then perhaps you are afraid of injury — but your bigger fear should be of being thought of as a weak player who not only can you not go to war with but who can also be crushed, simply because you avoid tackling. Is that what you want for yourself? Is that the reputation you want — of a weak player?

I know that you don't.

Well, that is why we're going to replace fear with drive and motivation. Basically what we want is to annoy ourselves a little so that we're all fired up inside. We want to ignite the inner fire that the fearless player has — the fire we already have within us.

We want to annoy ourselves in order to see how we've been awarding the fear we have just a little bit too much respect.

So your task for the coming week is very simple, and very easy too (if you could write this task down on a note that would be excellent).

Three steps for changing fear into drive:

Step 1: What does fear prevent you from improving on the field? (Be honest with yourself...put it down on paper.) Simply ask yourself, "OK, what scares me the most?"

Step 2: Write down what scares you even more than that. I want you to make yourself mad so that you'll understand that the fear that has had you shaking in your boots until now was actually nothing; insignificant. It was only in your imagination. Moreover, not only was it in your imagination, it was also a threat to your success. Do you really think that you're going to let something hold you back?

So step 2 is to jot down for yourself what scares you more than that fear.

For instance:

If you were afraid that if you didn't make it to the top league after all you've put into football, then tell yourself, "Maybe I'm afraid that after all I've put into football, in the end I won't make it. But I am more afraid of reaching the end of my career, looking at myself in the mirror, and knowing that I didn't try hard enough or give it all I had. So I think that it's important to give all I have to give today, because the efforts I make today are those that determine my future (my actions today create success, not concern for the future)."

Another example:

If you don't try to score a goal, because you're afraid of being yelled at by the coach and other players if you miss, then what you need to tell yourself is this: "OK, maybe I'm afraid to even try to score a goal and to be yelled at by the coach and other players if I miss — but I am more afraid of not giving my potential any chance of bursting out because I know deep inside that I'm worth much more than who I am today. So I'm going to take that kick from this day on (without hesitation) at every opportunity I have because the pain that I will feel if I don't try will be greater than the pain of maybe being yelled at by a few kids."

Here's another example:

If you're afraid of going to tryouts because of the odds of not being accepted, then tell yourself that, "Maybe I'm afraid of going to tryouts and of failing — but I am more afraid of sitting at home because at home I definitely don't have any chance of going very far."

Step 3: Do this at training today. What is that thing you've never planned to do because of fear, but that you will do every week because you're committed to yourself? What move have you avoided doing until today? Write it down or decide on it now — and do it today at training. Maybe today you'll take a risk and get behind players, or go hard for the ball, shout at the players without holding yourself back, speak to your coach about something that's been on your mind, try to score a goal in any situation, go for the first ball without hesitation, or attack without fear.

As long as your fear is there you are going backwards. Your breakthrough will only happen when you deal with the fear and act despite it. Remember, the best players are not those who are not afraid (they too are afraid, of that you can be sure) but they do not let it stop them, they go ahead anyway.

And now is the best time in your career to do it! Why?

Because it is what you chose to do!

You have the power to decide and to do it. I will give you dozens more techniques later on but you do not need more right now. What we do need is for you to go ahead and do what you know is the right thing to do — now.

So do yourself a favor and commit to:

1. Overcoming your fear.
2. Turning your fear into drive and making yourself mad by discovering a greater fear (which will make the previous fear seem like a mere fly on the wall) — simply explain to yourself that you've given too much credit to that fear that has been sitting there in your head until now;
3. Doing what is necessary during training this week to overcome it. To conquer fear means to say that from this day on you will know that even if your fear

returns (and it very well could), you are going to be strong enough because you've already overcome it in the past and as such there is no reason you won't be able to do it again.

My message in this chapter is very simple: Play with the fear, connect to it, and it will leave you — if you fight it, it will cling to you like a leech.

To make it easier for you I've done your work for you and prepared a few techniques to use to overcome the most common fears footballers have.

As such, I am going to give you new techniques, directions and methods to cope with:

1. The fear of losing the ball
2. The fear of injury
3. The fear of being yelled at by the coach
4. The fear of being yelled at by others (the fans, opponents)
5. The fear of disappointing yourself and others
6. The fear of playing on a new position and unfamiliar position
7. The fear of not being able to make a living from football
8. The fear of success
9. The fear of not falling asleep before a game (and coping with butterflies in your stomach)

10. The fear of talking to the coach (and of the coach's reaction)
11. The fear of switching teams
12. The fear of arriving late to a game

Are you ready to start?

We're going to get rid of all these fears and instead we're going to infuse our physical and mental muscles with the courage and hunger for success that we've been lacking until today.

Let's go!

1. The fear of losing the ball

The fear of losing the ball is one of the most common fears footballers have. And if we look within ourselves we'll find that beneath the fear of turnovers, there are other, greater fears, such as the fear of taking responsibility; the fear of receiving the ball and of making decisions; the fear of pushing up, or of shooting and missing; or the fear of being yelled at if you lose the ball. You could be afraid of the coach sending you to the bench because you lost a few balls, or of letting the fans down if you lose balls.

Let's stop now for a second and look at what all these fears have in common: If you look carefully you can see that the fear of losing the ball stems from the other fears that I mentioned.

Basically, if we break down each of these fears to the root of the problem, we'll reach the same point time and time again, and discover that the fear that concerns us the most is of feeling that we just aren't good enough. A player who is afraid of losing the ball is actually one who secretly tells themselves, "I'm afraid to feel like I'm not good enough and if everyone sees I lack talent they won't like me anymore."

What do we have here?

Instead of trying to overcome the fear of losing the ball, what you really need to overcome is your fear of not being good enough, or of not being liked. This means that…if you learn to like yourself and to accept yourself unconditionally, to feel like you are good enough, you can overcome this fear and any fear that may arise in your life.

How do we do this? Take note.

We've learned that the root of the problem is actually not the fear of losing the ball but of the implications of losing the ball (such as everyone seeing that we lost the ball, of feeling that we don't have what it takes, and so on).

So, let's take care of this fear and rid you of it entirely, just like you would remove an irritating app on your mobile.

In order to remove the fear, we're going to use our famous method of "turning fear into drive" (that we learned earlier in this chapter), and take note of how we're going to do it.

Our fear should not be of losing the ball; the fear that needs to drive us is of the game passing us by and of not even receiving the ball; of not being involved in the game.

Is that what you want?

Do you want to get to the end of the game without anyone noticing you?

Do you really want to play it safe and finish the game as an insignificant player...to not be noticed? I know that you don't.

You may have noticed that I'm trying to make you mad because one of the best and most efficient ways I know to overcome fear is to remind yourself that you are much better than you think, and since you're reading this book then this is the time to remind you that you really are a lot better than you think.

And if the fear of losing the ball is weighing you down, then that only says that you've forgotten to recognize your own worth. I want to remind you how strong you are. Even without knowing you personally, I know that you've overcome many obstacles. I also know that you've seen many players over your career, players who you've played with but who, unlike you, didn't last and they quit. When they quit you carried on and worked on yourself, because you believe in yourself.

So let me tell you a little secret — you are going to lose a lot of balls over your career.

And if you haven't lost any?

That means that:
a. You haven't tried to give any smart or complicated balls, in other words you haven't taken any risks (you've played it safe and boring).
b. You haven't received enough balls.

On the other hand, if you have received balls and lost them you're learning a lot more. Notice how many thing you can learn (and improve) when you lose the ball.

"I didn't think fast enough, I didn't let the ball go fast enough, I need to improve the technique of my more difficult balls, I didn't get to the ball fast enough, I wasn't focused on passing, I didn't prepare my body well enough to deliver the ball to its destination, my pass was too soft, or too hard, my first touch was too heavy, I thought too much before I received the ball to my feet, I was too cold to receive the ball."

Remember: Everyone makes mistakes — Messi, Ronaldo, Reus, Götze, Schweinsteige, Rooney...we could name them all.

The main thing that divides these champions from all those who landed up in the second or third league is that they learned from their mistakes!

Moreover, if I were to wish any one of my players anything, I would wish them to lose plenty of balls during their career and to learn from each ball that they lose.

In that way I know that if one of my players receives ten balls at the beginning and loses seven, then after a month they will receive 30 and lose seven. The odds are that out of the 30 balls, that player will deliver three smart balls that will position the main striker facing the goalkeeper — and that is the path to excellence.

The principle here is that at first you'll naturally make more mistakes, but the more you create opportunities for contact with the ball (in every situation), the more your body will feel comfortable and tell itself, "Hey, I've been here before, I know what to do!" In this situation the number of mistakes you make will decrease and your confidence and pleasure in the game will increase.

I'll sum up the bottom line with a sentence from Nike's last campaign, "Risk Everything" that delivered the following message using an animated Zlatan Ibrahimović, who said:

"If you fear making mistakes, you will play boring football. If you play boring football, you are no friend of Zlatan."

So you now understand that in order to improve you must lose the ball and take risks. In other words, you need to try to give different passes to in order to be of any significance and to have an impact on the field — that is how you can prevent yourself from becoming just one more uninspiring and uninspired player.

2. The fear of injury
The fear of injury is familiar and widespread.

Why?

Because it stems from the fear of feeling pain (and of even breaking something) and from the greatest fear of all — the fear of being finished as a player.

But wait, what kind of career will you have if you're afraid of injury?

What player will they see on the field? What achievements will you have? Let's talk facts for a little.

The game you have chosen to play is full of aggression, tackles, knocks, physical contact and a whole variety of injuries.

And that is part of the beauty of this sport. If we'd wanted to play less aggressively we'd have chosen a different sport.

Look at it this way — you now have the privilege of playing hard, releasing tension, getting into tackles… and it's all legal! That's football!

Let me tell you a secret that you already know — you will get knocked about quite often during your career, and you will even get hurt a few times.

And what will happen if you try to avoid physical contact in the game? You'll only expose yourself more.

In 2010, Nadine Kessler suffered a serious injury. She then moved on to become a key player for her team, Wolfsburg, and for her country, Germany. A few years later, when asked if the setback inspired her to achieve great things, she replied that serious injuries make you want to get up and carry on. Kessler also said that she saw things differently after being injured – she now enjoys every second of the game.

Nadine Kessler has picked up injuries on numerous occasions, which sometimes prevented her from playing and from training at important stages of her career. Yet, when asked about how she feels about these injuries, she is always very positive.

Nadine Kessler was the recipient of the FIFA World Player of the Year for 2014. When she received the award, she said that it was a reward for hard work, good performances and a good development track. She also felt that she would not have won it without her teammates.

In May, 2015, she signed a new one-year contract with Wolsburg.

Imagine a player in front of you who is afraid of tackles, who doesn't go for the ball and who always gives in when anyone puts the pressure on…you would smell their fear just like a dog smells fresh meat, and you'd have no mercy on them.

You would only wait for them to receive the ball and you'd send them flying with a powerful sliding tackle, you would steal the ball — and that player, who is going to get another 30 of those over the course of the game — will not mess with you.

The question is, would you want your opponent to see you in that way? I know that you wouldn't.

Your only choice is to play hard. That is how you'll mark territory, send a clear message to your opponents, make them doubt their own ability and try to get rid of the ball fast. They probably won't even try to test you with some creative dribble.

Tell me, do you remember Fabio Cannavaro from the Italian national team, the FIFA World Player of the Year? Cannavaro was tiny as a defender, less than 5 feet 8 inches (1.76 meters) tall! He overcame his lack of height with a ton of aggression, going to war over every free inch, tackling in every situation and from every angle, and mainly — he played with all his heart. This all brought him almost every title possible in football, including the FIFA World Player of the Year in 2006. Here's another story for you about fear and injury — **my own story.**

I'm sure you already know that my career ended as a result of injury — I tore my Achilles ligament twice, and I have not played since.

As one who has been through it — I do not regret a single tackle, knock, bump or icepack on my foot in my entire career.

Do you know why?

Because without fighting and playing hard I would have never made it into the great Maccabi Haifa lineup, with talented players such as Alon Harazi and Avishai Jano on the bench. Without uncompromising aggression, fantastic talent such as Avi Nimni from the outstanding Maccabi Tel Aviv FC would have turned my life into a circus in the wing and would have humiliated me in the semi-finals of the Israeli National Cup (which in the end we took).

Without giving the fight of my life, I would have never ever been able to cope with players like Aimar and Vicenteo from the legendary Valencia (who I played against in the EUFA Cup playoffs with Maccabi Haifa).

So don't worry about injuries — let your opponent worry about you.

How do you do this?

1. Play hard.
2. Fight.

3. Give your heart on the field — that is how you'll build a career without regrets, a career that you will never forget.

4. Play with the body language of a bulldog — even if you are not — I should mention that I am under 5 feet 7 inches (1.70 meters) tall…relatively short by today's standards, and I still built up a career on being an aggressive and passionate player).

3. The fear of being yelled at by the coach
Why are we afraid of being yelled at?

Maybe it makes us tense and distracts us from the game, maybe we interpret being yelled at as something negative? Maybe it makes us feel like we simply aren't good enough.

These are all true.

So, what is the good thing about the coach yelling? Try to imagine that you've made six critical mistakes in the game but nobody has picked you out. Have you lost out as a result? Clearly!

Why?

- Because you haven't learned what you're doing badly.
- Because you haven't improved or developed.

- You'll probably repeat the same mistake a 7th time, because if you don't see where you went wrong how can you prevent that from happening?

When you get yelled at by your coach (which is basically **constructive criticism at high volume**) you have two options — to close yourself off and to feel offended, or **to be a professional who always looks for what lies behind the words and searches for opportunities to improve.**

As such, from this day on, whenever the coach yells at you tell yourself, "How great is it that the coach is telling me these things. That's a sign of caring, of wanting me to improve, of wanting me to understand something that I don't quite get now."

"The coach has expectations of me? Excellent — I guess there is something worthwhile in me to see."

Don't get upset by the yelling — the coach is usually physically far away from you and wants to tell you something that you will hear above the other sounds of the game. The coach is also caught up in the whirlwind emotions of the game...just like you are.

By the way, what do you think happens in the higher leagues?

Why do players who make millions per season lower their heads and eyes and listen when they are being yelled at by top coaches such as Pep, Mourinho, Conte, Jürgen Klopp and others?

They accept the shouting because they know one simple thing —that their coach is a professional who is looking at things from the side.

If they have something to say, and they chose to say that something to you — it must be important, and you can probably improve as a result.

So if Marco Reus accepts yelling from Jürgen Klopp and looks for ways to improve, then you can most certainly do the same.

4. The fear of being yelled at by others (spectators, opponents) and how to overcome it

I have a question for you before we discuss this fear — how much attention are unimportant people given? None.

Nobody pays them any attention because they do not exist. They are invisible.

Another question:

People who make an impact...how much attention do they get? That's right, they get either positive or negative attention, but they are impossible to ignore.

There is only one clear conclusion to reach — if you are being yelled at by someone, it is a sign that you're important, you are making an impact, and you're in a position to make changes and to do great things on the field.

Your way to turn that fear into your friend and to help it help you to get ahead (pay attention — we're going back to it) is to:

1. Understand this simple truth;
2. Understand that the only yells and comments you need to listen and respond to are those of your coach.

Yelling by any other person has only one purpose — to distract you from the game.

Don't go along with them. Think to yourself how good it actually is that they are shouting at you and about you, know that you are significant and let those shouts fan the flame in your heart to play harder, with more confidence — because everything will then work out on its own.

Here is a true story: During the 1998–99 season, Alessandro Del Piero, then one of the greatest stars in the world, tore his knee, was injured, and was unable to play for a year and a half. During his comeback season, he scored only one goal. Nevertheless, he was invited to play for the Italian national team in the European summer tournament, EUFA Euro 2000.

Del Piero did not play much during the Euro itself, he was only a substitute and he was disappointing. But his high point came in the finals against France – when the score was 1:0 to Italy — and Del Piero carelessly missed twice against Barthez. France evened the score in the 90th minute and took the game during overtime. **Del Piero lost the Cup for Italy.** The following year Del Piero was the most highly criticized player of all in the league — there were signs cursing him being waved on every field, songs were made up about him and he was put down constantly during the entire game.

None of this stopped him from getting back into shooting shape with nine goals, and over time he became the top scorer in the history of Juventus.

Getting yelled at by the crowd?

Excellent, that means you're interesting, intriguing, you get people moving in their seats. It means that you're on your way to fulfilling yourself — so every time the crowd shouts profanities at you — enjoy it.

5. The fear of disappointing yourself and others

The greatest mistake that footballers make is that they judge themselves only on the results of the game, instead of on how much effort and work they put into it. Sometimes they also expect others to judge them in this way. All this can instill an overwhelming fear of disappointment in them.

And what do I mean...

Many players who are preparing for a game tell themselves the following: "They'll like me and see me as a successful person and footballer only if I'm good in today's game. If, heaven forbid, things don't go as well in the game today as I expect of myself, I'll disappoint others, and mainly, myself." That is not the way to prepare for a game in which you strive to demonstrate your best ability, and it is most certainly not the way to look at success in football. The truth of the matter is, your greatest success is that you are already in the profession that you love. The fact that you get up every morning and put all your energy into training, good nutrition, personal training – that is your greatest success.

Michael Jordan missed more than 9,000 (!) shots in his career. He was also solely responsible for losing more than 300 games. But does anyone remember that? Not at all. They remember him for the championships, for the All-Star games, his records and the Hall of Fame.

Was Michael Jordan a disappointment? No way!

External events can have an impact on our personal disappointment. In other words, there will be times in your career when you do everything right: You train hard, invest all that you have, and even demonstrate an amazing ability at practice – and still not get time in the game, not make the team that you want, or not be offered the contract of your dreams. The important thing at these times is to realize you cannot always control situations, but you can always control the choice between being disappointed or not. What am I saying? The following will illustrate to you what I mean:

When I was 19 years old, after eight years as a top player for the Maccabi Haifa's youth team, the time came to move up to the senior team. I was very excited. I had already started training with them, I had given the team manager my passport, I was imagining how happy I would be to begin the season with the senior team before the training camp in Germany, which would be starting just a few days after I got there.

I was so excited that I had already packed for the trip, bought things, told everyone!

Three days before the flight to Germany it happened… Itzhak Shum, the team's coach, and Yankele Shahar, the team's owner, called me for a talk. They did not even ask to speak to me inside; they called me over on the field and told me, "Eitan, we really value you as our player, you have proven yourself as the captain of the youth team, but we're sorry to tell you...you will not be continuing with us at Maccabi Haifa."

"Not continuing? Me? Why?" I said to them in a surprised voice, totally in shock.

"There are three others who play your position who are more experienced than you, so we're letting you go because you won't have the opportunity to play this year and we want and hope that you'll find a team that you'll be able to gain more experience with. Who knows, maybe you'll come back to us in a few more years."

Quiet; silence. I couldn't get a word out. I was completely unable to answer my throat was so dry.

Do you know that feeling, when you're so angry that within less than a millisecond you feel immense hatred inside and you don't know why? Well, that is exactly what happened to me. I found myself on the receiving end of the most painful slap in the face I had ever received. Here I was, only three days before becoming a Maccabi Haifa player, and in only two minutes of conversation under the sunshade, I was informed that as of the following day, I would have to find myself a different team.

I did not say a single word in that conversation. I was so hurt. I felt that my world had been destroyed. And along came the best friends of those who never make it — uncertainty and fear of the unknown — do you know them? They come visit us quite often in life, and always at the worst time possible.

I went home from that conversation with my face dragging on the ground. A period of six productive years with Maccabi Haifa had blown up in my face as if they'd never happened: "Go find yourself a team."

Luckily, even then I knew that it was time for me to find those hidden opportunities in the temporary disappointment I was experiencing, and I changed teams to Hapoel Ramat Gan, where I won the State Cup, a victory that would make Yankele Shahar sign me on for five years with Maccabi Haifa.

Here's another example.

Stephanie Roch's career has had its ups and downs. She represented Ireland at the youth level, but missed out in the final trials for Ireland's under-15s and was heartbroken. She carried on trying. She later made the under-17s team, and went on to score the winning goal during her under-19s debut.

In June of 2013, she was dropped from the lineup for a friendly game with Austria but did not let this hold her back in any way. She was determined to win back her place. After working on her game, Roch was called back by Ronan – the national coach – in October of the same year.

Stephanie Roch's goal in October, 2013 in the WNL for Peamount United was the runner-up for the 2014 FIFA Puskás Award for the best goal of the year.

Do you understand? As long as your self-esteem depends on results you will always fear disappointing others and yourself, and you will hesitate before every pass. In other words, footballers that judge themselves by the results of the game can expect their lives to be miserable and unstable because nobody can guarantee themselves they'll win all the time. On the other hand, if your self-esteem is based on the effort you make in every play – well, that's another story.

As soon as you understand that you can never be a disappointment as long as you put everything into every play, your life will change and your ability will improve immediately. This is because your true victory actually lies in the efforts you put into every play over time. Winners are not those people whose lives work out quickly for them – they are those people who value themselves and like themselves for the effort and work they put in on their way to the top.

Disappointment is the result of too-high expectations – if you expect every single one of your plays or games to be perfect, you are setting yourself up for disappointment. And naturally, when your own expectations of yourself are too high, you also think others have the same expectations of you.

What's the solution?

If you change your too-high (and irrational) expectations of yourself, you can permanently change your ability! (And guarantee that you won't be disappointed.)

So here's what I want you to say to yourself before the game: "As long as I show great determination and effort in every play I make, I am content and happy with myself. True, if I am determined in every play, my success is still not guaranteed…but if I'm not determined, I will certainly not succeed in every play. The effort I make does not have a bad day. I always give every play 100%, and when I make an effort and put my heart into it, there is no way I will be disappointed because I base my self-esteem on the effort I make, which is under my control. I cannot always control the results. Today I realize that it is unrealistic for a footballer of my level to expect a perfect game; I am a player who knows that mistakes are the most important stage on the way to success – I love who I am, and accept myself as somebody who also makes mistakes. The mistake is not what's important. What is important is how quickly I choose to recover from mistakes and to get to the next play with enthusiasm.

6. The fear of playing on a new and unfamiliar position

Many football players see new positions as a drawback and a reason to feel pressurized, whereas the best football players in the world see a new position as an opportunity for further success.

"How is that possible?" you may be asking. Well, here's a story to illustrate why playing on another position is the greatest gift you can receive as a football player aspiring to fulfill your dream.

I'd like to take you back to the Fifa World Cup of 2014, and to behind the scenes of the Netherlands national team. To be more precise, to the third game between the Netherlands and Chile. Until that game, the national team's coach, van Gaal, was not happy with his left defender – Daryl Janmaat. He decided then to put his backup plan into action, which determined that the team's main striker, Dirk Kuyt, would play as the left defender in the game against Chile. To remind you, Dirk Kuyt, the striker who had scored so many times for his teams (Feyenoord, Liverpool, Fenerbahçe) was suddenly called on to play a position he was not used to playing.

While the other players were concerned with the radical change in positions (after all, a move from being the main striker to being a defender was not a natural one) – Kuyt saw this as an opportunity. Moreover, not only did Kuyt have no fear of this plan, he even liked it. In the game against Chile he played well and was stable, the Netherlands won 2:0, and van Gaal used the same plan in the quarter-finals against Mexico.

In the quarter-finals, Kuyt started off in the left defender position and then switched to the right defender position. Crazy, right? A player who had scored so many goals for his teams (Feyenoord, Liverpool, Fenerbahçe) was not afraid of being *the* player for his coach. I read in an article that Kuyt had said, "If we want to do well, we have to go van Gaal's way…"

What happened here?

Kuyt was focused on only one goal – to succeed in football and to help his national team succeed, no matter what position he was placed in. The ego of other footballers would have objected and said things like "that's not my role!", "I'm being made the laughing stock of this team!", "I don't enjoy football anymore!" And they would have made other childish statements of footballers who have not yet matured.

To get back to Kuyt and the Netherlands – The Netherlands won 2:1 and made it to the quarter-finals against Costa Rica. Kuyt played right defender for 120 minutes with an accuracy of 88% in passes. The game ended with a tie score of 0:0 and the Netherlands won 4:3 on penalty kicks (and needless to say that Kuyt scored one of the penalties).

In the semi-finals he played for another 120 minutes as the right defender against Argentina but this time the game ended with a loss in penalties. In the match for third place against Brazil, the Netherlands won 3:0, with Kuyt playing in the right defender position for 90 minutes.

The bottom line? Here are Kuyt's statistics in the Fifa World Cup: five games as a defender (left and right) – only one goal was scored against the Netherlands in the 510 minutes that Kuyt was on the field playing defense.

Dirk Kuyt serves as an example that proves that if you're required to play on a new position, your first response should be – enthusiasm and hunger. Why? Because this new position is an opportunity for you to:

1. Accumulate more experience – dozens of practice sessions can never equal a single game.
2. Increase your financial worth as a footballer – clubs are willing to pay more for diverse players capable of playing on more than one position.
3. Gain more game time. Do I really need to expand on that?
4. Improve your understanding of the game: A new position naturally forces you to improve your spatial vision and the way you've viewed the game until now. When you understand the demands of your new position you automatically become a player with greater odds of success;
5. Receive more exposure. (I am yet to meet a bench player who is surrounded by journalists when the game ends.)

So, are you still afraid of playing a new position?
If your answer is still yes, do the following:

1. Learn the principles of the new position you're meant to play (go into YouTube and watch players on the position you are meant to play).
2. Ask your coach exactly what is expected of you.

3. Write yourself a note stating what plays you need to focus on in order to play a stable game (not perfect – stable).

To sum up, to play on a new position is like learning and knowing another language. And just like someone who learns a second language is able to communicate with more people in the world, so you too, when you are able to play another position, will increase the odds of becoming a footballer who more people know and love.

7. The fear of not being able to make a living from football

To address this fear, I need to ask you something. Tell me, do you know of any jobs that guarantee your success in that field?

Do you know of any singers, businesses or TV programs that guarantee success in advance? You and I both know that the answer here is no.

But here is the thing with the fear of not being able to earn well.

Footballers who fear not earning well enough are typically those players who are preoccupied with thoughts concerning what could go wrong – while the players who succeed are relentlessly busy with improving all physical, professional and mental aspects. As such,

most of them are concerned with self-improvement –
they do not have the time to stop and think about what
could go wrong.

In other words – movement beats fear.

Every time you feel scared of not earning enough from
football, what you're feeling is a sign that you are thinking
too much and not practicing enough. Concerns are a
hidden signal telling you that you are not really going
all out in your career. Concerns are a hidden signal that
you are preparing a Plan B for yourself, and that kind of
approach to achieving success doesn't work.

The right approach to dealing with this fear is to
understand that this fear is not fear, it is your personal
friend (just like a personal trainer) who shows you that
you need to invest more in order to increase your odds
of succeeding.

So today, you basically understand that you do not have
a thing called fear of not being able to make a living from
football. What you have is an inner buzzer that wakes
you up whenever you start to invest less in yourself.

When you're occupied with improving yourself, you
will not have the time to worry.

To sum up:

If you focus on making a living – you will delay making a living.

If you focus on self-improvement – you will make more than enough.

8. The fear of success
The fear of success is a very common fear among athletes worldwide.

The first question that comes to mind for you may be, "How can we be afraid of something that is considered good?"

So the truth is, success (just like the lack of success) comes with a price.

Here are some examples and reasons why footballers fear success:

The fear of change: The fear of having to cope with new, unfamiliar and unknown situations when you succeed – such as dealing with a new team that has better, more professional players when you have no experience dealing with players of a higher level; or, the fear that, if you succeed, you'll have to give television and newspaper interviews when you have no idea how to give an interview. You may feel things like, "I'm good at what I do but not at public speaking – that scares me," or "If I succeed, then my coach and team will have higher expectations of me – and I don't know how to carry all that responsibility that I have all of a sudden." Usually this fear stems from a lack of experience, skills, or knowledge in certain areas.

There is also the fear that we ourselves will change, and that we won't recognize ourselves or that we'll no longer like ourselves.

The fear of commitment / the fear of losing your freedom: For some footballers, spontaneity, variety, hanging out with friends, and the freedom to do "whatever they feel like" is important. They may be concerned that success will lock them into a boring and rigorous training regime, diet, planned sleep schedule – and that as a result they will suffer from boredom, loss of spontaneity and of enjoyment.

The fear of responsibility: A successful person often bears responsibility for themselves and for other people who depend on their success, such as their coaches, teammates, club owners, etc. The fear of not being able to bear this responsibility over time, of having to think twice about every step and move they make as they may affect other people, is what leads to their fear of success and to the desire (often unconscious) to forgo it ahead of time.

The solution here is very simple. We need to increase our belief in our ability to handle any challenge that success brings us. In other words, the winning belief says that "if there is a footballer who has a successful career and who still has an enjoyable way of life, then I can too."

The name of the game here is to achieve balanced success! Balanced success means that you can have your cake and eat it too. You can work hard at football and enjoy time with your friends too (by creating the right dose of get-togethers with your friends). You can eat things you like and maintain your desired weight (by simply determining with a dietician how many treats you can have).

You understand? The idea is to maintain balance, and balance means that you can allow yourself to live with a new approach and line of thought that says that "success doesn't mean that I have to give up anything. To the contrary – it only shows me that I am ready to carry on with the same things that I like, simply in the right doses, and as such I am ready to deal with any change."

9. The fear of not falling asleep before the game
The fear of not falling asleep is often the result of having too many thoughts, most of which are expressed as questions that you have running through your head. Examples? "What is going to happen tomorrow?", "Am I

going to be smiling at the end of this game, and what will happen if not?", "This is the moment I've been waiting for all week – I hope it doesn't go wrong for me."

What can you do?

Firstly you must remember that your goal before a game is to make sure your body gets optimal rest time, at least eight hours, and preferably you should go to sleep between eleven pm and midnight, not at one or two in the morning. Every hour of sleep is important so your body receives enough rest before the game. As such, we need to understand that thinking too much before a game gets us nowhere. All it does is tire us out.

So here are a few techniques that will help you fall asleep more quickly and increase your confidence:

1. Breathing: We have a tendency to stop breathing before a game (or before an important event). When your body lacks oxygen it enters a state of stress and that is why you feel more and more distressed and cannot sleep. Therefore, take five deep breaths (or more if you need them). When you inhale, check that your stomach rises and swells, and when you exhale, check that your stomach drops. Five such deep breaths guarantee you a sense of peace, concentration, and you may even find yourself smiling and feeling self-confident!

2. Imagine two successful plays you've made. Simply take a few deep breaths, put your earphones on and listen to a song that you like. Imagine two successful plays that you want to perform in the game. I would recommend imagining one defensive play and one offensive play. This will help your body to feel confident and release some of the pressure your body is under now.

3. If you still cannot fall asleep, go to the kitchen and eat something small and sweet. I always liked to eat a slice of whole grain bread with honey. Another choice could be a date or a banana.

4. If you still can't sleep, then turn your fear into drive. The way to do this is by understanding that you don't really need to be afraid of not falling asleep before a game. What you really need to fear is going to sleep without feeling excitement or butterflies in your stomach – most people who don't feel excited that tomorrow is their day, are usually the people who have jobs they don't like (unlike you, who loves what you do). I will never forget when I had breakfast one time with my colleague Avram Grant. I asked him, "Tell me, Avram, weren't you nervous before and during the UEFA Champions League final, when you were Chelsea's manager?" He answered, "Tell me Eitan, which is better – pressure and excitement at the UEFA Champions League final, or peace and quiet at home without ever knowing how far you

can go?" He went on to say, "I learned to love the pressure. Today I feel pressure if there is no pressure on me or no exciting aims." So I want to pass Avram's message on to you. The feelings you have before a game are absolutely natural. The pressure is actually not really pressure; it is a feeling of preparedness in your body, as your body gets ready for your next task – the game. Therefore, each time you feel butterflies in your stomach, smile, breath and know that you're exactly where you should be – excitement before a game is a natural stage that every successful athlete experiences. Don't run away from it – love it.

10. The fear of talking to the coach

A footballer who is afraid to talk to the coach is usually one whose status in the team is unstable: a bench player, somebody who swings between the lineup and the bench, or a player who doesn't get as much game time as they would like.

This fear usually stems from the fear of "How will the coach react if I ask to talk? With anger? Will I make matters worse by asking to talk?" The fear of making your situation worse is a real fear.

So, here is the way to speak with your coach with confidence, and to ensure that you receive the answers that will advance you personally in the team.

When you want to talk to your coach, your aim is firstly to approach this in a way that says, "I would like you to help me improve," not one that says, "Why am I not in the game!" Understand that when you approach the coach and ask why you're not playing, there will always be a reason because your question is worded negatively. On the other hand, if you ask the coach, "Coach, what can I do to improve and to make the lineup?", your question is worded in a way that requires a practical answer that will explain what you still lack in order to become a leading player in the team.

Things to emphasize and key points to pay attention to when you talk to your coach:

1. Aim to receive specific answers: When the coach tells you, "You need to be more aggressive," that is still not a clear enough answer, so ask further – "What can I do that will help you see that I've become more aggressive?" In this way you are obliging your coach to look for professional actions that will help you to understand what you need to do to improve, and when you receive answers such as "stick to your player like glue when they go deep into the field," "take a highball with determination and don't pass on the responsibility to someone else to be there to take your place." Can you see the difference between a general and a specific answer? Try to get instructions,

a recipe, tools that you can use to help you change your behavior in practice and in games – that is the secret behind change.

2. Initiate a discussion on your own, and come to the discussion on your own, not with representatives such as parents, agents, etc. If you aspire to become a leading football player then you don't need escorts. Practice leading yourself and from the moment you decide to talk to your coach, be the one to run the whole show.

3. Remember that the coach is a human being just like you are. Don't turn this into a big deal. Remember that your goal is the same, to succeed as a team, so when you enter the room the coach will see that you are both on the same side.

11. The fear of switching teams

The fear of switching teams is one that is expressed through one main concern, which is: "The fear that I won't fit in socially and professionally with my new team."

Switching teams means new friends, a new coach, possibly a different playing style, and these are all elements that may concern a player who is considering moving to a new team.

As such, the only, truly important characteristic that you need to develop and use when you switch to a new team is: adaptability. That is basically your ability to adapt yourself to your new team's playing style and approach, while maintaining your own playing style and personality – a challenging task, but a possible one.

Here are the steps that will help you to make a smooth transition to a new team:

1. During the first practice sessions, try to learn as much as you can about the coach's demands and personality. That way you will be able to fit in quickly with any plans. (Note, I know that you want to make an impression with your playing style, but the only impression you need to make is to prove that you're a diverse player who knows how to read your new coach's way of thinking and to play according to their principles.)

2. Be friendly in the locker room, but draw limits and have respect and self-esteem! In other words, this means: Be yourself and don't try to change, but be friendly and try to talk to your teammates. This will lower your stress levels and increase your self-confidence at practice.

3. Focus on your professional actions, and remember: You are in football in order to get ahead. You're not here to be in the limelight, so make sure all your attention is focused on improving your professional actions – not on trying to please your teammates.

Every play you consider making – make with certainty. If you want to try to score – kick! Don't hesitate. If you make a decision to pass, and you know that it's the right decision even though someone has shouted to you from the other side – follow your instincts and make the pass that you decided on. Be determined in your 1 v 1 defense – players that are new to a team tend to show too much respect and don't play aggressively enough (due to their desire to fit in socially and to avoid rejection or being ignored by their new teammates) – wrong! The truth is that the more aggressive and determined you are, the more respect and esteem you'll receive and that is your goal. Remember, you are aiming to be a successful player. Practice with determination and with intensity; as if you've already been with your new team for five years.

4. Stay after training for individual work on the elements that you need to improve.

5. Watch recordings of the team's previous games – they will help you to learn your new teammates' playing style.

Something to consider: Don't ever rush to switch teams. Moving to a new team can be very easy, and players who aren't making one team's lineup tend to move to a different team due to their motivation and belief that they will play more in a new team. What they don't realize is that they are taking themselves and their habits with them to the new team; and a player with poor practice habits cannot improve overnight by moving to a different team. Therefore, if you are considering switching teams ask yourself one question: "Do I practice today like a lineup player even though I don't receive much game time?" If your answer is yes, and you're happy with the fact that you aren't going to be guaranteed an easy battle in a new team, then go for it – you are mentally prepared to switch teams. If you know deep down that you're not giving your best, my recommendation to you is to improve and increase your training level in order to make the lineup in your current team.

12. The fear of arriving late to a game
The fear of arriving late to a game is one of the easiest fears to deal with. I'll tell you more than that – it is even an unnecessary fear because you can easily avoid it.

I remember when I was playing for the Maccabi Haifa youth team, and my father would always make sure I arrived 45 minutes before the team was set to meet. At first I would get angry at him and say, "You see?! We're too early again! We could have left later and I would have had more time to sleep." Now, in retrospect, I am grateful for the education he gave me, because I understand that arriving early allows you a calm and quiet start to the day of the game, without the unnecessary stress felt by players who arrive at the last minute on game day.

To arrive on time, you simply need to create the conditions necessary to prevent you from being late.

Here is a method for always arriving on time and for never being late.

1. Get your game bag ready the day before (so you're not leaving everything to the last minute).
2. Set an alarm clock. Ask your parents or partner to set theirs too.
3. Know how you're getting there: organize a ride to the game the day before. If you're traveling alone, that's excellent. If you're being picked up, make sure you know where the pickup point is the day before, and call the person taking you an hour earlier on game day.

Successful players and people take responsibility for their success. Punctuality is fundamental to your success so make being on time a standard and habit in your career.

Use fear as a positive tool to get you going. If you need to, and I highly recommend that you do, read this chapter again and go over your exercise every day for the next three days. That is your task for the coming week. Now is the time, and today could be your day.

Next time you feel something, an instant before you call it by some name such as fear or stress, change its name to focus, challenge, opportunity — because the truth is, those feelings passing through your body indicate that something good is about to happen.

Now it is your turn. I've worked hard in this chapter, so now it is your turn to reap the benefit.

Your task is very simple:

1. Choose one fear that has been disturbing you until now.
2. Read the instructions for coping with that specific fear — and turn it into the drive for success.
3. Go to training sessions and see how easily you make the move that you were once afraid of.

In the next chapter, you will learn how to stop being concerned with what others think of you and how to stop any background noise or negative thoughts from undermining the confidence you need when you play.

Chapter 9

How to Stop Worrying about What Others Think or Say about You behind Your Back

We have reached one of the most important chapters you will read throughout career.

Today you are going to learn how to stop being concerned with what others think of you during the game and how to prevent a yelling coach or spectators from undermining your confidence and impairing your personal ability during the game.

If you adopt and use all three rules and the method I am about to teach you, at the end of this session you will be able to go onto the field for practice or games with a clear head. You will be relaxed with the ball, and you'll reduce the odds of losing the ball by at least 50%. You'll double the number of positive actions you perform in the game and you'll create a name for yourself as a reputable footballer who is valued and respected by your team.

On the other hand, if you don't adopt and implement the principles I am about to give you here…if you allow what others think of you to affect your ability…then you can expect to live a very unstable life as a tentative player who has too many concerns and fears.

In other words, if your mind is going to be occupied all the time with what other players or the coach thinks of every pass or move you make — you'll be distracted, you'll have a hard time recovering fast from mistakes, you'll lose the ball, and you won't fulfill your potential. This will happen not because you're not good enough but because your fear of receiving negative criticism and of disappointing other people will be in control of your mind and will distract you by making you think that you need to show peak ability.

Because we do not want that to happen to us in our career, it is vital we know how to free ourselves of any concerns regarding what others think of us. In this chapter we are going to do it together so that nothing will threaten your career success.

Let's start.

In order to show your real capabilities in every game and every practice right from the start, without worrying about what others think of you, I am going to teach you what big mistake makes us worry about what others think of us and of our abilities.

The critical mistake I am talking about is "assuming" — or in other words — guessing (and believing yourself) that you know what the coach, spectators or your teammates think of you. You simply start to believe that you can read the thoughts other people have (when in effect you don't really know what is really running through their minds.). However, because you need so much positive feedback, when you don't know what other people think of you, you start to guess.

To help you understand what a devastating trap assuming is to your professional success, I'm going to share a short story to help you get the idea.

Ashley asks Jordan out and they plan to meet at a restaurant at seven in the evening. Ashley, being polite, arrives at six forty-five, takes a seat and waits for Jordan to arrive. Time passes, and there is no sign of her. He remains calm and tells himself, "Well, she still has time, it isn't seven yet."

It is almost seven and Jordan is still not there. Ashley is still composed, and once again tells himself, "Well I'm sure she just wants to be fashionably late so she can feel important and hard to get, that is why she isn't here on time — she's playing with me."

Time passes, and now it is already seven fifteen.

Hmmm…now Ashley is starting to get mad and irritated — "What a nerve! She has no shame! I've been waiting here for half an hour already and she's still not here, who does she think she is?"

That, however, is only the beginning. At seven thirty Jordan has still not arrived, she hasn't texted him, she isn't answering her phone — nothing. Ashley is getting really mad now. "I cannot believe she's playing these games with me and treating me like this…does she think I'm not good enough for her??? I'm done with her," he thinks to himself. He shoves his chair away from the table and leaves it in a really bad mood.

And then…a moment before he angrily leaves the restaurant, Jordan arrives, out of breath and ready to drop.

Ashley sees her and without allowing her to say a word, gives her a piece of his mind.

"You should be ashamed of yourself, who do you think you are being so late? I thought you respected people,

I've been waiting here like a dog for 45 minutes…you and I are through."

And then, just as he's about to leave, Jordan tells him, "I was ready and just about to leave to be here on time when at six thirty my mother fainted, and I immediately called an ambulance. We sped off to the hospital, and because I forgot my phone at home I couldn't call you, so I took a cab here from the hospital so that you wouldn't think that I didn't care about you, oh…and my mother is fine, by the way."

At that moment, Ashley was left speechless, started to turn red, and did not know where to bury himself he was so embarrassed.

What do we have here?

Ashley made assumptions — how so? He saw that Jordan wasn't there on time and immediately made up a negative story: "Look at how she's playing games with me," (even though he had no idea what was happening).

After fabricating this negative story, he started to believe it too. When you make up a story, you also start to believe it — so what you're doing, basically, is filling yourself up with emotional poison that overwhelms you with anger and irritation.

This is followed by a reaction — and how did this Ashley react to Jordan? With ugly aggression that made him look like a total idiot in the end. It isn't that he wasn't a good person, but that he had filled his mind with negative stories and lies that had never happened. All they did was make him feel worse about himself.

But wait a minute!

Why am I telling you this story, and what does it have to do with your success as a footballer?

Because when you assume that you know what others think of you, all you're really doing is making up stories that never happened because until you ask, you don't really know what anyone thinks of you. We footballers have a tendency to assume everything, from what their teammates in the locker room are saying about us to what the spectators think of us, even though we don't actually have any real idea if what we think is true or not.

This, however, is where our troubles only begin, because the real problem starts when we start to believe our assumptions are true. That and more — when we start to believe our own stories we can actually swear that they are true. We take things personally, get hurt and start to blame others, react aggressively— and create a great big drama for no reason at all.

Ashley could have thought to himself, "Well maybe something happened to her," or "I hope she wasn't hurt in an accident," but he didn't. Instead, he took it in a negative direction because that is what people do. They take things personally and think that everything is against them.

Footballers make assumptions, just like Ashley did, and that impairs their ability.

Because what often happens to us in football, without us even noticing, is that we start trying to read what others think because we're looking for their approval.

Here is an example that I come across often, something that may have happened to you too.

Say that you've given a great game, you've been excellent, you were number one on the field…and at the end of the game the coach didn't tell you how great you'd played or have anything good to say to you.

Well, if you were to jump to conclusions, what you would say is, "What? Why am I getting no positive feedback from the coach? Maybe I didn't play that great? I'm no good — what a drag."

You come to practice the following day with your head hanging, you demonstrate poor ability because you're sure the coach thinks nothing of you. In response, you take no notice of anything the coach says, which makes the coach think that whatever ability you demonstrated in the past had been false, and in the end you're removed from the next game's lineup.

Now, take note of what happened here. After giving a great game and not receiving a good word from the coach, you jumped to the conclusion that the coach thought nothing of you. What's the real story here? The coach had been ill with the flu for two weeks, was having a really hard time, and had still come to the team's training sessions and games to do everything possible.

Do you understand how much poison you can feed yourself when you assume and believe your assumptions? By trying to get into the minds of other people and to read their thoughts, you're causing yourself terrible suffering!

So why do we assume? Why do we make up stories and try to guess what others think of us, when in effect we don't really know what the truth is?

The answer is quite simple. Our brains, our minds, want us to feel confident all the time. Our minds want us to be in control all the time. Our brains are always trying to connect the dots.

For example, you could be absolutely sure that your teammates don't like you because they don't send any passes your way, when in truth, they may want to pass to you but you never make a good move into space. So you could think that they don't like you, when actually what you're missing is self-examination and awareness of how you're not doing enough to make a good movement off the ball into space to receive the ball.

Here's another example. You lose the ball and immediately look at everyone, absolutely certain that they are thinking that you're weak, even though something completely different is going through their minds. You could lose the ball and your friends could encourage you after the mistake and tell you that it's not a big deal, move on, and despite their encouragement you can still tell yourself that "they are just saying that, I bet that inside they really hate me right now."

Our brains are very interesting and we footballers have the need to justify everything all the time. We want to feel certain and if we don't know something we will make up a story just to fill that knowledge gap so we can feel safe.

There is something important you should know about your brain, because it is critical to your success.

Why doesn't it matter if the story you make up is true or not? Your brain wants you to feel that it is in control of things and basically, by giving your brain an answer you are making yourself feel in control, and that is the reason we make up stories...to feel good with ourselves. The problem is that we sometimes don't see how the stories we tell ourselves turn into poison, which makes us feel bad with ourselves, impairs our ability and lowers our chances of having a successful career and of breaking through to the next level.

What happens when you make up stories in your mind... when you're sure that everyone is against you — and you start to believe it? You begin to react aggressively to whoever you think was thinking badly of you, and when you react aggressively or automatically, you make a new enemy for yourself; one who never had any previous intention of hurting you.

I want to share something that happened to me. When I was 25 years old, I played with Maccabi Herzliya. I was awarded the captain's armband by the team's coach Freddy David.

Freddy and the team's management truly valued my professionalism and hard work, and decided to make me captain.

Sounds great, right? To be 25 years old and captain of a team in the premier league. Not bad.

The problem was, I was a young player when I received this promotion and I was worried about what others thought of me. Although I had no idea if they supported this move or not, I began to run scenarios through my mind.

I won't forget how, before my first game as captain, I entered the locker room and looked at all the players. At first I tried to read their thoughts and guess what they were thinking of me.

And then thoughts started to run through my own mind, such as, "They think I am too full of myself now," (although that would never happen, but that didn't stop my mind from making up all this nonsense).

And then, "I bet they won't play well today just to ruin my first game as captain."

I looked at the players who were older than me and told myself, "Look at them talking behind my back," and with those thoughts how do you think I responded to and treated those around me?

That's right!

I was distant!

That is the worst thing a captain can do.

And I started that game in the worst way possible. I was distracted, I lost balls, and I checked constantly to see who was looking at me and who wasn't. I'm happy to say that I then did what I'll soon be teaching you to do to stop anything from distracting you from the game.

Do you see how we can ruin our entire career, simply by believing the stories we make up in our heads?

When we believe something, we are so sure we are right that we're capable of ruining our relationships with our friends and coaches to protect our position.

That is almost what happened to me with my teammates, only because I assumed. Sounds minor — but that minor thing is a critical mistake for our ability.

Why does it happen?

Because sometimes, when we're so self-involved, we assume that everyone else sees life just like we do. We assume that others think what we think, feel what we feel, make decisions just like we do and hurt others just like we do.

That — precisely that — is the worst assumption (the gravest mistake) a person can make, and when they do, they become afraid of being themselves with others. We think that everyone will judge, victimize, mock and blame us, just as we ourselves do; before others have the chance to reject us, we reject ourselves — that is how the human consciousness works.

We also assume things about ourselves, and by so doing we get into an internal argument with ourselves. You may find yourself thinking, "I think that I can give a good game," for example and later you are disappointed when you can't. You may think too much or too little of yourselves without being realistic — but why does that happen? It happens because you haven't taken the time to ask yourself questions and to answer them. It could be a good idea to get more facts about a given situation and it could be a good idea to stop misleading yourself over what you really want.

Often when we're in a group there are things we don't like and we then try to change others. The problem with this is that people change only if they want to, not because we can change them. The trick is to accept other people just the way they are without trying to change them. If we try to change them that means we don't really like them.

So, how do we solve this and stop doing it? How do we stop the crazy nightmare we are creating for ourselves?

Here are three rules that will free you from worrying about what other people think of you; rules that will help you to play and train every day with a mind free of pressure. When you bring these rules into your life — your career will completely change!

Rule Number One: Never assume

Don't ever tell yourself stories that you don't know are true. If you assume you are only creating a dark place for yourself in a reality that does not exist.

From this day on, stop trying to read the thoughts of others and stop assuming that you know what they think of you. If you don't know something, ask. If you think people are saying negative things about you — find out, but as long as you don't know what has been said about you or thought about you, don't assume.

Rule Number Two: Work with the facts (not with stories)

If you see that you're starting to make assumptions that send you spinning off into imaginary scenarios, and you're beginning to tell yourself dismal stories, ask yourself one smart question: "Is that really true — is what I am telling myself right?"

For instance, say, you lost the ball and you tell yourself that the coach thinks you're hopeless now.

Ask yourself the following: "Does the coach think nothing of me because of one lost ball?" Usually, the answer will be a resounding no! That isn't true. Return to reality, go back to taking care of those things you do have control over, and to the next play that can get you ahead on the field. That means that if you're in the middle of the game, go sprinting back to your position, run to steal the ball, communicate with the players around you, live the game. The game will go on, with or without you. When you catch yourself telling stories and foreseeing a dark future you need to stop and return immediately to reality.

Rule Number Three: Be who you are and don't wear masks

This means that you don't have to change for any particular team or for any particular person! You need to be who you are and if that doesn't suit some people, it is their choice whether to be your friend or not.

Think about this for a moment. I don't know if you've ever watched the TV reality show *Big Brother*, but if you have, have you noticed what type of people usually win? Who are those people who usually take the million? The answer is very clear. The ones who win are those who do not pretend to be someone else, with themselves or with others. The winners of these types of shows are usually not concerned with what other people think of them — they are concerned only with what they think is the right thing to do.

I'm not a great fan of *Big Brother*, but I am an enthusiast and a dedicated researcher of human behavior. I have used *Big Brother* as an example because it is clear there who is wearing a mask and who isn't. This is usually the rule — someone who is honest with themselves and with others is the one who the audience likes and sympathizes with, who receives tens of thousands of text messages each day from the millions of fans in any country it airs in.

Why does that happen?

Are they all good looking? Attractive? Talented? No!

It is because people connect to real people.

People can see through false people who wear masks.

Just like TV spectators like to like real people, so football spectators, coaches and other players will like you if you let them see the real you. You want people to like you and to relate to you. That will happen when you show your true self and stand up for yourself, which means shouting during the game if you don't agree with the ref's call, it means going all out for every play or pass that you decide to give because when the players around you see that you're determined, what they will say to themselves is:

"Alright! Now that's a player who knows what they are doing," and they will be there with you, cheering you on, but even if they don't, you don't worry about it because you know that the play you wanted to make was right. As such, from this day on you will go around with an attitude that says, "Take me just the way I am — you're free to take me or leave me," or in other words, "If you like me the way I am great – I'm all yours!"…"If you don't like me the way I am that's fine, I'll see you around, you can find yourself someone else."

This may sound too tough, but it really isn't, all it says is that you talk to people very clearly and that helps other people understand that they need to accept you just the way you are.

After all, you can stop yourself from worrying by stopping to assume and by starting to feel comfortable in your own skin.

How can you do that?

1. What you don't know for sure is happening, is not happening! If you have no proof or real evidence that what you think is true, it remains untrue until it's been proved right.
2. If you aren't sure of anything or you don't understand it — ask. Find the courage and ask questions until you are able to see things clearly, and even then, don't assume that you know everything you need to know about a given situation. After you hear the answer, you won't need to assume anything because you'll know the truth.
3. Don't be afraid to say what you want either. Do not be embarrassed to share your feelings. Everyone has the right to agree with you or not, but you always have the right to ask and to receive answers. Not only that. Everyone has the right to ask you things and you have the right to agree or not.

If you don't understand something it is better to ask and be sure than it is to assume. On the day that you stop assuming communication will become more clear, pure and free of emotional poison. When you stop assuming you will become more honest. That is the rule. Do not make assumptions. That may sound simple, but it isn't always easy to implement. It isn't easy because we are often programmed to do just the opposite. Our habits and routines are inherent in us, without us even being aware of them.

Becoming aware of these habits and understanding the importance of this rule is the first step, but it is not enough. This knowledge or concept is only a seed implanted in your mind — action is the main thing.

OK, so now is your time to act and do everything you can to reach the prime of your personal ability in the game, which will take you to the next level of your career.

This is what you need to do next —

When you're at practice or at a game, I want you to start paying attention to your thoughts and to your brain's attempts to read other people's thoughts. As soon as you catch it red-handed inventing some story (that you don't know really happened) or trying to imagine what other people think, I want you to stop. How? By simply saying to yourself: "Stop, I'm making things up. The only thing I care about right now is what I'm doing." If you do this well, you'll see how your mind will be free of negative thoughts and you'll find yourself with a lot more air and calm on the field.

I have prepared a personal letter to help you follow your own truth:

It doesn't matter what people do, feel, think or say — I am not going to take anything personally.

Today I realize that other people will always have their own opinions that match their belief system, and as such anything they think of me is not about me — it is about them.

I control my own destiny. Today I choose to deal with myself and not with what I think others want me to be because I know that the only recognition I need in life is the recognition I give myself.

I am capable of recognizing those times when I am occupied with other people and those when I am occupied with myself. I also know that just as a stone cannot shine without being polished, so a person cannot be perfect without being judged and observed.

It is the nature of people to make fast judgments, to criticize, make remarks. That is OK by me because I play for myself, I am living my own dream and not the dream of others — at all times.

Chapter 10

How to Show the Same Ability in Games as in Practice

In this chapter you will learn why the need to play perfectly in games makes us feel afraid, impairs our personal ability, and ensures the end of our careers before we even make it. It will also talk about how to ensure that this won't happen in your career. In other words, our aim in this chapter is to make sure that you begin each match with the right attitude, which will help you play a relaxed game, receive the ball calmly, play with confidence and show the same abilities that you show at practice.

I work with a lot of footballers that I would define as perfectionists. They are those players with very noticeable characteristics, the most noticeable being their tendency and desire to play perfectly in every match. They are also the players who have to have everything go according to plan. They need every pass to reach its destination, to make no mistakes, for every move to look good, and to never have anything bad said about them.

My experience shows that there is a very, very strong connection between the need to be perfect and the fear of failure in football and in sport in general.

In other words, there is more chance of perfectionist athletes demonstrating poor ability in games.

I'm sure you're asking how this is possible. After all, being a perfectionist and aspiring to being perfect in this game is a good characteristic that should help us do well in the game, no?

Well, not exactly.

The truth is, because perfectionist football players are such highly motivated athletes, their motivation leads them to believe that the way to succeed in their career is by demanding perfection of themselves in every game, and no less than that.

As I am sure you know, the expectation to be perfect makes a person subconsciously set their goals too high — so high that even Messi would not be able to achieve them. A player who expects to play perfectly in every game is usually the same one who becomes frustrated and loses confidence when they don't fulfill their own expectations during a game (we'll talk about that soon).

The trademark of perfectionist football players is that they usually invest more time practicing than anyone else, but for some reason they never manage to show the same ability in games.

It is ironic that those players who train the hardest and put so much into drills are usually the ones who are overwhelmed by the fear of failure.

Why does that happen?

One of the reasons is that perfectionist players fall in love with training. Because being good is so important to them, they sometimes forget what their real career goal is.

The true goal in football is to use your training to succeed in games, not vice versa

But perfectionist players are so busy improving themselves in practice that without them even noticing it becomes their main career goal.

Then, when the game begins, they believe that anything less than a perfect game or victory is failure.

Do you see where we're going here?

Don't get me wrong, it's not that I'm telling you that aspiring to be perfect is a bad thing, but I am telling you that being a perfectionist has its pros and cons. The pros are excellent, but the cons are devastating to career success.

As such, in this chapter we are going to find the right balance together; the balance that you need to go onto the field and to play freely, with the same ability that you demonstrate in practice — and even more.

The first stage in finding the right balance is first to see if you have a tendency to perfectionism, so we're going to do a small test. I want you to read the following three sentences and to see if you identify with any one of them.

1. My need to be perfect in a game makes me miss my true goal — to play with confidence and to be of use to my team.
2. It is so important to me to be perfect that any tiny mistake frustrates me and makes me see myself as a failure.
3. Even though I spend hours training, with the aim of becoming a successful footballer, during the game I cannot perform to even a quarter of the ability I show at practice.

Have you read these sentences?

Do you identify with any of them?

If the answer is yes, then you are in the right chapter, because our aim today is to understand how the need to be perfect and having (too high a dose of) desire and motivation is why the fear of failure overwhelm us.

How does the need to be perfect make us tentative and afraid of failure during the game?

Football players with a high work ethic are those players who not only put physical effort into training, they also invest a lot of emotional effort that makes them want to win so badly that as a result they set their expectations of themselves too high. A player with too high expectations of themselves will find themselves feeling very frustrated with themselves very fast — when they do not fulfill the expectations they set for themselves.

What can we do?

We want to learn how to separate between our aspiration to be perfect in training and our expectation of being perfect in games (which leads to our fear of failure).

In other words, what we want to do is to identify which too high expectations or harmful habits we bring with us to the game, and after we've pinpointed them, we want to work to change them. That is how you'll step onto the field with the right thoughts and approach, which will help you to demonstrate that true ability that you know you have.

We are therefore going to perform two simple stages:

Stage One: Identify the too high expectations we have of ourselves.

Stage Two: Change these expectations into winning goals that we are always able to achieve and as such feel better with ourselves. Our bodies will feel more relaxed and our plays will flow just the way we want them to. (By the way, we will achieve what we secretly expect of ourselves through these new goals.)

If you implement the following exercise you can expect to feel a fast change in the way you think, and moreover — you will be able to see that you are breathing more easily after doing this exercise.

So let's get started.

The first stage, which will help you begin each game with a smile, confidence and fearlessness, is to see if you have any tendencies to perfectionism. If there are any signs that you're a perfectionist we will exchange those tendencies with other habits and you will very quickly find it quite simple to run onto the field stress-free and to enjoy it too.

So let's get started.

I want you to read the next few points, and I want you to write down in the margin, which three signs you most identified with (three behaviors and thought patterns that you feel happen to you in your career):

1. I love training. The truth is, my confidence is very high at practice but when I go onto the field my confidence drops because I feel more comfortable at practice.
2. I am too preoccupied with the final score of the game (and not with my ability). I am so preoccupied with the final score and with winning that my brain automatically starts to think about the possibility of losing, and the negative reactions I'll get if I lose. That makes me play tentatively, makes my legs and other parts of my body feel heavy and tired, and I become distracted during most of the game.
3. I am too preoccupied with what others think of me. I worry about being criticized by others. I am concerned with disappointing people if I don't win, and I if I don't fulfill my own expectations my self-esteem will really crash.

4. It is important to me not to let anyone down, and I want to fulfill the expectations that people have of me. It is important to me not to let my parents, my friends and my coach down.

5. I feel it is important to show perfect ability. I am sure that I will perform well if I plan every move I make in the game, and yet trying to plan every pass and play of the game prevents me from playing a relaxed game (because I am constantly thinking, and that makes me tired). Other than that, my need to control every move sometimes makes me lose faith in my own ability.

6. I want to perform with perfect ability so that the coach will continue to include me in the lineup and that makes me make mistakes and overwhelms me with fear.

7. During the game I am occupied with the mistakes I have made in the past and that makes me play more tentatively, avoid the ball and not try any new plays because I am afraid of making more mistakes.

Are you finished reading?

Great.

Did you find out anything new about yourself?

Did you notice where a tendency to perfectionism hurts you and impairs your ability?

Excellent (I mean excellent that you could identify where).

Now you have three modes of thought and behavior written down that you think create the most damage.

The fact that you have them in front of you already proves that we've made a significant step towards your success, because now you are aware of the habits that possibly make you fear failure, which is what makes your body feel tense and stiff.

The identification stage is critical for change to occur because that is how you will be able to recognize the next time your mind starts to set your expectations too high, which is a good time to change your approach.

However, to create a change in your approach you need to know what you need to change.

That is what Stage Two is about.

After you've pinpointed what you need to change (that approach that you were about to take onto the field with you) what you do next is —change your way of thinking.

The first change you need to make in your way of thinking is to differentiate between aspiring to perfection at practice (which is extremely good for us) and the expectation to be perfect in games (which is terrible and destructive for us).

In other words, the aspiration to be perfect at practice is excellent. There is no problem with aspiring to make every pass accurate, or to want every play to work — that is OK because you're training, and the purpose of training is to demand of yourself that you reach high levels of perfection in every drill.

The problem is that you cannot demand perfection of yourself in a game, because it is simply unreasonable, and if you try to be perfect in games you will automatically sabotage your ability because there is no such thing as a perfect game.

However reasonable it may sound to want to be perfect, just the opposite is true, and the need to be perfect is detrimental to your motoric ability and your belief in yourself (we'll talk a lot more about believing in yourself later).

The disadvantage that perfectionism causes to your career is that it automatically makes you set demands on yourself before a game that are too high and unreasonable, which is what makes you worry about what other people think of you and preoccupied with statistics and winning.

As such our goal at this stage is to understand that striving for perfection at practice is excellent, but expecting to be perfect in a game is destructive.

In other words, being a perfectionist is not bad; in fact it's even good. Perfectionist football players have excellent qualities such as a high work ethic, self-discipline, a strong will to succeed. These are qualities we wish to use but at the same time we do not want to demand or expect perfection in our performance during the game.

The most important thing that I want you to take from this chapter is this:

Perfectionism is the lowest standard of success

Demanding perfectionism from yourself in a game is a SILENT KILLER **for your career**

By now I'm sure you're asking why. Well, when your life is your career and you demand perfection from yourself in every game, what you're basically doing is making yourself feel constantly bad with yourself.

When you demand perfection of yourself in every game, you are being like that irritating judge who is always noticing what you're not doing well in, where you haven't done enough yet, where you could have given more and you didn't — and yes, you can always give more, but if you don't reward yourself for small successes then you will always feel that you aren't good enough. That is destructive to your self-confidence. Don't get me wrong — not being a perfectionist does not mean stopping to work like a dog and stopping to demand hard work of yourself at practice. Not at all! It means that you continue to keep a high physical and professional standard in training —but when you get to a game change your way of thinking. At games you will want to think slightly differently from the way you have been thinking on the days before games. Because of this change, you will perform at a level of ability that you've always dreamed of. This change is not physical. It is a mental change in your approach to the game. To be more precise, it is a change in your expectations of yourself.

To make it easier for you I've prepared a table that looks like this:

Weekly Mental Preparation Program						
What to Think about on Each Day of the Week to Attain Peace of Mind, High Confidence and Peak Ability for the Game						
Day One	Day Two	Day Three	Day Four	Day Five	Day Six (The day before the game)	Day Seven (Game Day)
Time for rest, analysis and recovery		Time to work hard and to strive for perfection			Time to let go and trust your body	
Your approach: It doesn't matter if I won or lost the last game, I will not judge myself on a bad game, nor will I celebrate like crazy over a great game. My body and mind need to recover now, so today I choose to take the time to rest, to be honest with myself, to take the good and to commit to improving those points I need to for the next game (without taking shortcuts) because I know that this is the only way to get ahead professionally.		Your approach: I aim to train today and to perform every play well. I am highly motivated to conquer the field and to improve every parameter of my game, I am committed to persisting in order to achieve my career goals and today I choose to demand more of my body than I have ever demanded of it before! Today's training session is the most important moment in my career!			Your approach before a game: Today I choose to blindly trust myself and my body. I will follow my instincts because I am confident in the training I have done. Today I will stop judging myself and analyzing my ever move. Today I choose to be tolerant, to focus on the "here and now" and not on the future, and I have no problem with ugly wins —I even like them! Today is the day that I am going to allow my body to do what it wants to because it already knows how to shine on the field and how to perform at its peak ability!	

I would like to go over this table with you to help you understand how to use it and how you can attain the ability you have always dreamed of by using it.

So, as you can see the table is divided into three columns.

Game Day is Day Seven on the table, which includes a seven-day training plan.

Days One and Two are devoted to resting, analysis and mental recovery (unless you didn't have a game on Day Seven and you can then do more intense training), but from a mental aspect it is important to take a different approach at the beginning of the seven-day period and to tell yourself the following:

> It doesn't matter if I won or lost the last game, I will not judge myself on a bad game, nor will I celebrate like crazy over a great game. My body and mind need to recover now, so today I choose to take the time for myself to rest, to be honest with myself, to take the good and to commit to improving those points I need to for the next game (without taking shortcuts) because I know that this is the only way to get ahead professionally.

Days Three, Four and Five are days to go all out and to devote yourself wholeheartedly to training. The middle of the seven-day period is the time to work hard and to strive for perfection, so your approach needs to say the following:

> I aim to train today and to perform every play well. I am highly motivated to conquer the field and to improve every parameter of my game, I am committed to persisting in order to achieve my career goals and today I choose to demand more of my body than I have ever demanded of it before! Today's training session is the most important moment in my career!

And then we get to the most important of the seven days – **Day Six and Day Seven.**

These are the days that most players continue to work hard and to try to be perfect —but not you. Today you know that the way to play without holding back is by simply trusting your body, throwing your expectations to the wind and trusting your ability, because your body is such a clever machine that all it needs is your support.

As such your approach for these two days should say that the day before and of a game is the time to let go and to trust your body.

So on the day before the game tell yourself:

Today I choose to blindly trust myself and my body. I will follow my instincts because I am confident in the training I have done. Today I will stop judging myself and analyzing my ever move. Today I choose to be tolerant, to focus on the "here and now" and not on the future, and I have no problem with ugly wins — I even like them! Today is the day that I am going to allow my body to do what it wants because it already knows how to shine on the grass and how to perform at its peak ability!

I am a human being and together with the good plays I make during today's game, I will also make mistakes. That is OK. As such, I am committed to aspiring for perfection in training, but I will continue to accept that I cannot be 100% perfect in games. How great it is that I now know that expecting myself to be perfect in training is excellent but also, that it is unreasonable in a game. That is why, now that I give myself permission to make mistakes and to recover from them quickly, I feel much better because that says that it doesn't matter what happens today, I am committed to playing for myself and to enjoying this game, because my talent will only shine through if I enjoy myself, and giving everything I have to give — that is true victory.

That is it for this chapter, and at this point, I would really like to congratulate you.

You have gone through a significant stage in your development, and you can see that by truly meaning these words when you read them, you are now smarter and mentally stronger than other players. Now your aim is to train and to live out this approach.

To put it simply, what we have learned in this chapter is that you can demand perfection in every play you make — when you're training. Not in games. Game time is when you need to blindly trust yourself, trust the training you did, and be patient with and nonjudgmental of yourself. Don't put yourself down, love winning in every situation, even if it's through plays that don't look that good. An ugly goal is a goal. An ugly save is a save that could secure the game.

Let's move on and play in order to be effective, not perfect. I suggest you take the rest of the day off before moving on to the next chapter. Our aim is not to finish the book but to make a real change and upgrade to your ability, so be proud of yourself, take time off.

I will be waiting for you tomorrow in the following chapter.

Chapter 11

How to Play with Confidence Game after Game: The Formula

In this chapter, I am going to wrap this all up for you and send you off to every game, week after week, with peak confidence in yourself. In other words, in this chapter you are going to learn how to develop your number one tool for success in your career — self-confidence — and how you can take it with you onto the field, game after game.

We both know that it doesn't really matter how much talent you have, or how hard you've trained. The most important asset that separates the best players from the others is self-confidence. You simply cannot compete and reach the top or fulfill the true potential that you have in your feet without having confidence in your talent and ability.

About 90% of footballers who come to me do so because they want to build up their self-confidence or regain it after they have lost it for some reason. What I see is that many players want to have self-confidence but most of them don't realize or understand what self-confidence really is, or how to increase it.

With some 20 years of experience in football, I have found that to reach the top and to stay there, players need to develop and work on their confidence, just like they work on any other ability such as kicks, air balls, in the gym or going 1 v 1.

As such, in this chapter you will learn what self-confidence is and how you can create it. You will be given powerful techniques to build and improve your self-confidence. You will learn what mistakes you need to watch out for so you don't fall into the traps that send the confidence of most players crashing.

I will teach you how to prepare yourself for every practice and every game so you can start every game with peak confidence from the moment your foot touches the grass. You will learn how to feel comfortable with the ball when it comes your way.

The thing is, if you take these tools and methods that you're about to receive and implement them you will be able to start every game and deliver every pass or kick without hesitation. You will get behind players fast or be more determined than your opponent in 1 v 1. You will be able to go home after each game or from practice with a smile on your face, a sense of satisfaction, appreciation and respect from other players and your coach — and all this unrelated to whether you won or not.

Still, there are players who will never learn about or use the tools you're going to receive here, and they will never be able to show the same ability in games as they do at practice. Those are players who remain "practice players" for life. I know that you don't want to be one of those because you are serious about developing your career.

Therefore, I propose you take the next 15 minutes for yourself, switch off or silence your phone and anything else that could disturb you. I promise you, if anyone is looking for you or wants you, they will still be there later on to drive you crazy.

Let's get going.

OK, so the title of this chapter is "How to Play with Confidence Week after Week — the Code to Winning." And talking about self-confidence I would first like to say that self-confidence is not easily defined. If I were to ask you now, "Tell me, what is a trophy?" I think your answer would be something like, "What is a trophy? Well, Eitan, clearly a trophy is a piece of gold-painted metal and the one who wins first place gets it."

OK, and if I were to ask you, "What is a ball?" What would your answer be then? Again, I assume you would tell me something like, "Eitan obviously a ball is made out of inflated rubber covered with strips of leather or plastic and it is used to play the most popular game in the world, football."

OK, good. You've answered both questions well.

But…

If I were to ask you what self-confidence is, what would you tell me?

Hmmm…when we talk about self-confidence we are talking about something intangible, something that cannot be touched, and suddenly we have no idea how to imagine it. Although we know how we feel when we feel confident, we don't really know how to explain this thing we call self-confidence.

I want to put things in order here, because self-confidence is intangible. It is not some object that you can go to the store and buy whenever you get the urge!

So what is self-confidence, you're asking?

Self-confidence is that feeling of being sure of yourself, and the best way I know to define it is like this —write this down (in your head):

Self-confidence is how strong your trust in yourself is to perform an act or task well.

Self-confidence is when you know that you can succeed in any situation you choose to act in.

Self-confidence means the real confidence you have in yourself, the knowledge that everything depends on you alone, and that you determine your own fate.

In other words, when you have self-confidence you trust yourself 100%, you are certain that what you want to happen will happen without the need for you to perform any conscious thought process — precisely that is self-confidence.

Let's take everything I've said about football and let's try to understand just what self-confidence is in football.

Self-confidence in football is a sense of certainty that the play you're going to perform will go well, even before it happens.

I'll repeat that:

Self-confidence in football is a sense of certainty that the play you're going to perform will go well, even before it happens

In other words, self-confidence is when you know that you're going to do something well before you do it.

For instance:

- Self-confidence is when you know that the pass will reach its destination before you've cleared the ball.
- Self-confidence is when you trust yourself to get behind a player before you have done so.
- Self-confidence is when you feel that you're going to net the ball before you even kick.
- Self-confidence is when you know that you're going to steal or stop your opponent's ball when it is coming towards you before you take it.
- Self-confidence is when you feel comfortable when the ball is coming towards you, when you know what you're going to do with it and nothing puts you under pressure at that moment. In other words, when you trust that the next move you want to make will work —that is self-confidence.

And this is exactly what we're going to learn how to do. In only a few more minutes you are going to know just how to achieve a frame of mind allowing you to make every pass without hesitation and with a sense of certainty and true knowledge that the ball will go where you want it to; that in every 1 v 1 your opponent will feel threatened, not you; and perhaps, and maybe more importantly, you will learn how to control your feelings and your negative responses so that no mistake can reduce your faith in yourself — that is confidence.

So, what have we learned so far?

We have learned that self-confidence is a feeling, a sense, a trust in yourself and in your ability, a belief that your plays are going to work! Not only are they going to work, you also know that they will work before they even happen…that is self-confidence.

I'm sure you're asking yourself now, "OK, Eitan, I get you, and I get that confidence is like a sense in my body that allows me to perform without fear, but how do I build up my own?"

As always, your question is excellent.

Before I can teach you how to become highly self-confident, I need to first teach you that football players have two types of confidence:

The first is true confidence.

The second is false confidence.

1. **True confidence** is confidence that truly builds up your sense of security.
2. **False confidence** is when you use things that you think will raise your sense of confidence but they actually only lower it without you noticing.

We're going to discuss each of them so that you can learn how to develop true self-confidence and stop falling into the trap of false self-confidence.

What is true confidence?

True confidence is when you focus on what you can control. In other words, when you focus on your ability, on your good qualities and on actions and moves that only you can do for yourself, such as:

- Running
- Training on your own after practice
- Shouting out and talking during the game
- Eating well
- Consulting with professionals to help you to improve
- Taking risks when passing another player
- Passing
- Making a backward pass
- Deciding to go forward without quitting after giving the ball away

- Trusting your body to perform the next play well
- Encouraging yourself after you make a mistake
- Drinking two glasses of water each morning
- Silencing the voice of the "critic" who is trying to break your concentration

From a very young age, Abby Wambach was determined to succeed. When she was only 5 years old, she was transferred to the boys' team after she scored 27 goals in only three games.

Wambach was toughened up by her brothers who fired hockey pucks at her for target practice. As the youngest of seven children, she had to compete to succeed. Her siblings never let her win. She had to be better than them to do so.

Wambach always knew that there will always be someone who is better, and so she worked on her own technique. She began to work on her technique as a young player in her hometown, Rochester. As a pre-teen, she started to elude defenders by heading the ball over them and then running round them. She worked hard to perfect her game, staying after practice to work on diving headers – a skill that later became her signature as an international player.

Thanks to her tenacity and hard work, Abby Wambach won two Olympic gold medals and the 2012 FIFA World

Player of the Year. She has won the U.S. Soccer Athlete of the Year award six times and regularly makes the lineup of the U.S. women's national team. In May 2015, she was included in Time Magazine's Time 100 list as one of the 100 most influential people in the world.

In other words, true confidence is when you don't wait around for something to happen so you can feel good with yourself. It is when you act in advance and do things that are in your control in order to feel good with yourself in every situation.

What is false confidence?

False confidence is when you focus on things that are not under your control. In other words, false confidence is when you tell yourself things like, "If the weather is good I'll feel confident"…"Good feedback will boost my confidence"…"If the referee will be on my side I'll feel more confident."

Now, all these things are out of your control! When you focus on them and trust in them you are misleading yourself, because these are not things that you have any control over.

In other words, the greatest mistake that undermines our confidence and our ability on the field is putting our trust in things that are not under our own control. For example:

There are players whose confidence is boosted only when the coach gives them compliments. In other words, there are players who feel confident only when the coach throws them a good word.

Why is this problematic?

The problem here is that you do not control the feedback you get from your coach. In other words, let's say that you've just given a great game; you were incredible, number one on the field. For some reason, however, the coach didn't say a single good word to you during the entire game, and you know what…not only that, but at the end of the game, the coach simply drove off home.

Now, if your self-confidence depends on feedback from your coach, or in other words, if your confidence increases when the coach encourages you, then what would happen in a game like that Yes! Your confidence would hit rock bottom as fast as an elevator with a broken cord would drop from the 50th floor.

Now just between you and me…should your self-confidence have crashed because you didn't receive good feedback in that game?

Not at all! After all, you gave a great game! And you know that you did…so why does your confidence drop anyway?

Because you are basing it on external factors that are not under your control.

You have set a rule in your mind that your confidence will only grow when you get positive feedback from your coach. Between you and me, feedback from your coach is not yours to control…and as such…if you aspire to get to the top in your career, you cannot build up your confidence on the basis of the coach's feedback because self-confidence is what you feel when you know on your own if you've been good or bad. You don't need anyone else to tell you because you can do that yourself. You can give yourself the appreciation that you deserve when you're good. On the other hand you can also shake yourself and improve when you need to. As a footballer who is aspiring to succeed you want to start paying attention to situations in which your confidence depends on things that are not in your control.

There are players whose confidence depends on the weather. If it's a nice sunny day, they feel good about themselves before the game starts…but if it rains or the field is no good, all their confidence dissipates.

Now, my question to you is this: Do you control the state the field is in? Not at all, just like you do not control your opponent.

Being concerned with the condition the field is in makes your confidence drop if the field is no good. By the way, if the field is in good condition, and that boosts your confidence, then the confidence that you're feeling at that moment is merely false confidence because the purpose of confidence is to make you feel confident in yourself on any field, unrelated to the condition it may be in.

Here is another example, and this one you may be familiar with…

There are players whose confidence goes up only if their first pass of the game goes well and reaches its destination. If they lose a ball at the start of a game it's "the end of the world" as far as they are concerned, and they then expect a bad game.

Now…say that you got to the game extremely well prepared, you did everything you needed to do, you slept well, ate well, did all those things that are in your control, but the coach of the opposing team instructed four players to go for you as soon as you got the ball and to steal it from you.

Is there a possibility? Sure! I know quite a few coaches who instruct their players to close down on their opponents as soon as the game begins.

So sure, you are in control of your passes but you can't always start the game perfectly, and you may lose the ball right at the start, even if you're really focused.

What we want to make sure of is that a lost ball, which is part of the game, doesn't lower your confidence because it's OK to lose a ball. It is not OK to lose confidence because of that lost ball because your confidence does not have to depend on that last pass. Your confidence is built up over years of training and games and as such from this day on I want you to start evaluating yourself not only on one game, or on whether your last play worked or didn't, but on the many years that you've been playing.

Take David Trezeguet from France. Remember him? He played for Juventus and for France's national team? He won the FIFA World Cup and countless championships and cups? If you don't remember him, let me remind you and tell you a little about what confidence can do for a player.

Trezeguet was a very limited player. All he was good at was kicking and headers to the goal from the penalty box. But each time he received a pass from outside the penalty box or any time he had to go down a little to help the team move the ball, he would mess up. In other words, every time he left his comfort zone (where he felt the most confident), he would lose a lot of balls, make mistakes, send balls into the stand, get mad at spectators, but…everyone knew one thing — in the end Trezeguet would score.

It could be an empty-net goal; it could be a header from the arc. The ball could hit five players and eventually drop at his feet right in front of the goalkeeper. It didn't really matter. It was clear to everyone that in the end, Trezeguet would score.

How do you think he reached the stage of playing for a full 90 minutes? The answer is simple:

Trezeguet's self-confidence was so high that he refined the characteristic top main strikers need, called a "short memory." Their short memory does not allow them to let mistakes or failure lower their confidence. Trezeguet realized the magic of a short memory…and if you've ever followed one of his games (and if not I recommend you watch him on YouTube or find a full game from his time with Juventus), what you'll remember is that after every one of Trezeguet's unsuccessful plays, after every lost ball, after terrible passes, after anger and curses from the spectators for his misses, he would simply forget about it as soon as it happened, turn over a new page, run to make a move to dead space — as if he had never made a mistake before in his life.

If that move also didn't end in a goal, he would run again (for the 100th time if necessary) to one of the far posts in case some stray ball happened to come his way (or he would try to break the offside again).

What was his secret? Trezeguet's secret was that he did those things that were in his control. He didn't care what the spectators said; he didn't care if it was snowing, hailing, raining or blindingly hot. He wasn't interested in who the opponent was, which defender was marking him, which game he was playing. Nothing.

And Trezeguet's results? Note:

Trezeguet scored 138 goals for Juve in 245 appearances. That comes to 0.56 goals per game, which makes Trezeguet the top foreign scorer in the 116 years that Juventus has been around. Trezeguet also won the FIFA World Cup, the UEFA European Football Championship, two French league titles, the Serie A — the Italian Football Championship — twice, the Supercoppa Italiana – the Italian Super Cup...twice. He was awarded the Italian Player of the Year and the French Player of the Year, and was the Serie A Top Goalscorer for 2002.

He did all this even though he could not pass outside the penalty box...that is the power of self-confidence and self-trust.

So we have now discussed both types of confidence: true confidence and false confidence, and what we have seen is this:

True self-confidence is when you're thinking about the things that you control, such as your ability, your training, eating well, your belief. When you think of the good practices and games that you've had, when you imagine the success that you want for yourself...all that is under your own control.

False confidence is when you're preoccupied with those things that you do not have control over (and these are the things that your confidence will no longer depend on after today):

1. An unjust call by the referee is not in your control.
2. Feedback from friends is not in your control.
3. Feedback from your parents is not in your control.
4. Your opponent is not in your control (and should therefore be of no interest to you anymore!)
5. Your competitors for the lineup are not in your control!!

6. What the newspapers say about you is also not in your control!!!
7. The weather is not in your control.

As such what we want to do from this day on is to pay attention to what we focus on, and to make sure that our confidence is based only on what we have control over, because self-confidence is what we have when we deal with those things we do control.

That, by the way, is the reason that this type of confidence is called self-confidence — because it is confidence in yourself, and if it is yours that goes to say that the only way to boost your confidence is to do only those things that you have control over, without waiting or expecting anything that you don't control to happen.

A player can wait for a great team to sign them but it is not under that player's control. What they can do is make that team notice them. How? By training, improving, standing out and maintaining their stability in every game. That is what'll make that team notice them.

One of the things I would really like you to understand here is that self-confidence is not something we're born with, in our careers or in our lives in general. It is something that we build up from one practice to the next, from one game to the next.

So let's start building up your confidence.

You could listen to me now, get really excited and tell yourself, "Wow, this is great stuff," and then go to practice and go right back to those same old habits that you had before, without implementing the techniques you will be receiving here. I am sorry to tell you that if that happens you will not learn a thing.

Again, I will say:

You may get really excited over the tools and material you receive in this book, and then despite your enthusiasm go off to practice and not implement any of the tools you've been given here — and you may think that you've learned something but in effect if you haven't made any changes at practice, if you don't do something different on the field, then you have not really learned anything.

As long as you haven't changed your behavior…as long as you haven't changed your behavior on the field…not only have you not moved forward on a personal level, you have even gone backwards.

What we're going to do, because we don't want that to happen, is we're going to build up your self-confidence through action on the field — starting today.

Self-confidence increases when you persist in doing those things that you control. That is the only way to gain experience, and experience, as you know, leads to…confidence! And confidence leads to success!

The good news is that self-confidence is not something we're born with, it is something we build up from one practice to the next and from one game to the next.

So let's start building it up now.

The way we're going to build up your confidence is from the inside out, or in other words, we are going to build up two types of confidence: internal confidence and external confidence.

Internal confidence is the kind that makes you believe in yourself and that gives you a sense of capability.

In order to succeed, however, it isn't enough to think positively and to feel good, your body needs to believe you too, and as such what we want to do is to build up your external confidence as well.

Our external confidence is basically the body language that we use to convey to the world that we are confident in ourselves. To convey to the world that we're confident means that we want to look and behave at practice and in games like players who always feel highly confident.

Naturally, the two complement each other.

Internal confidence and external confidence each consist of four stages.

We are going to start by developing the four stages of our internal confidence.

Stage One of Confidence: Accept Yourself Just the Way You Are

When I say that you should accept yourself as you are, what I mean is that the first condition for boosting your self-confidence is to admit who you are and to accept yourself along with your weaker sides...those things you would quite happily give up. This means loving and respecting your whole selves even if you are not the "perfect package."

Why do we need to do this?

Because only when we accept ourselves just the way we are is the door to improvement and change open to us. As long as we do not accept ourselves and are not prepared to accept our own imperfections, we remain blind to the truth. When we try to ignore the truth, we do not have a true way to measure or evaluate ourselves.

When we don't know how to evaluate ourselves realistically, we start trying out new things on the field or things that we're not that good at. Doing new things (that we have no idea how to do) is the number one mistake and has an immediate negative impact on our ability, making others, such as the coach or other players, lose their trust in us.

I'll add a personal example. When I was younger I realized that my best abilities included agility, moving fast from my spot, accurate kicks, physical strength, physical fitness and tenacity. The abilities I lacked were in 1 v 1, dribbling, and not being as tall as the others. When I got to the great team Maccabi Haifa, I was suddenly exposed to players who could get behind their opponent as if they were thin air, and I was tempted to try to do things the way they did. I did know, however, that those were not the things I was very good at, so I had two options to choose from. I needed to either focus on what I knew best, or to try to improve those things I wasn't very good at.

My experience had taught me that to become a prominent and unique player (who attracts attention) you need to first focus on the things that you're good at, and to make those things your calling card. That doesn't mean that you don't work on those things you're weaker in. Clearly you'll need to work on your weaker abilities in order to get ahead. But...and this is important...your goal is to invest most of your time during the week to practicing and getting better at those things that you're good at, because that is what makes you unique, and that is where your competitive edge over other players comes to light, even if on paper they are considered better than you.

I remember my first season with Maccabi Haifa when I was up against the toughest defenders there were. The two Maccabi Haifa defenders then were Alon Harazi and Avishai Jano, both role models and legends in Israeli football whom I'd supported as a child. All of a sudden, I found myself competing against them for a place in the lineup.

What happened then was that a "small voice" (and the coward) in me woke up, and it did not allow me to accept myself as I was...there was a side of me that was constantly searching for what I wasn't good at and for what I lacked. I found myself telling myself things like, "I have no experience, I don't have Harazi's height, and I don't have Avishai Jano's audacity. All I am is a young player who has just signed with the senior team. I'm an unknown...I haven't been here long enough — what chance do I have of playing this season?"

There was also a winning "strong voice" in me — the voice of confidence — that could see that I was the best

I could be despite the competition. That strong voice said, "Eitan, listen up. Maccabi Haifa didn't sign you because of your pretty eyes, you're here because you've proved that you deserve to be, you are fit enough to play for two days running, you're tenacious, your passes are clean and accurate, you know how to get free when your opponents are closing down on you, you already have everything you need to win any battle over the season's lineup."

Which voice do you think I chose to listen to at every practice? You got it! The strong voice that accepted me for who I am.

This approach is what got me into the lineup that season. I played in 25 league games including in the EUFA Cup playoffs, one against Valencia.

I can tell you that there is no way that would have happened if I hadn't accepted myself and liked myself just the way I was, because whether we want to or not, we have a relationship with ourselves and our bodies are listening to anything we tell ourselves or think about ourselves.

As such, your aim today and every day, is to tell yourself, "I like who I am. That is the way I am and it's great! There are all the reasons in the world for me to succeed, and with the talent and ability I have right now I am going to win."

And on the subject of height, take Messi for example... small as a flea and yet still the best in the world. Or take Emanuele Giaccherini, who is also short at under 5 feet 5 inches (1.67 meters) and who at 24 was playing in Italy's fourth league, yet within five years was playing for Juventus and for Italy's national team. We could even go so far as to take Tevez or Ribéry who are not exactly great looking, and as you know a person's appearance can have a strong impact on their self-confidence. If Tevez or Ribéry hadn't accepted themselves for who they were, do you think they could have got to where they are today? Clearly not, because if you do not accept yourself then your body doesn't accept you, and if your body doesn't accept you (if you're ashamed of yourself), then there is no way you'll feel comfortable showing what you're really capable of.

So next time you look in the mirror, accept yourself and like who you are because you already have amazing qualities that will help you to go far.

Stage Two of Confidence: Imagine Yourself Succeeding at Least Once a Day

Why? Because both our physical reality and our goals are formed twice:

The first time in our minds…

and the second time in reality.

Without first imagining, no goal can be accomplished. The imagery stage builds up your confidence in your mind!

Players with high self-confidence have a winning image of themselves. Successful players do not wait for the right moment to feel good, nor do they wait for the right moment to simply occur spontaneously. Successful footballers feel good whenever they choose to. How do they do that? They imagine themselves doing well before they actually do, and through the simple act of imagining their body experiences the success they want as if it has already happened and they feel good with themselves. When the game starts, their body already remembers the feelings created by their imagination, and that is precisely why they feel comfortable with the ball, hold their heads up high while moving the ball, pass without hesitation, are determined to score — and that is precisely what you want too.

I'll give you a personal example of how using imagery helped me in difficult moments.

I used to travel by bus to the Maccabi youth team practices. Imagine the oldest bus possible, black clouds of smoke spewing from the exhaust pipe (a bus so old you could feel the smoke seeping into the bus). Imagine the bus being over packed with people of all ages, young and old, children shouting,— and add to all that an irritable driver who curses half the time and slams on the breaks every five minutes making you feel sick.

Let's say that these are not ideal conditions before football practice. I realized very quickly that at that rate there was no way I could arrive prepared to train, and if I didn't come prepared I would never be able to prove that I belonged in the lineup, and if I didn't play in the lineup I had no chance of making it to the senior team.

This is where imagery comes into the picture. During those difficult moments on the bus, I would take out my Walkman (yes, even the Discman wasn't out yet and smartphones were not even a figment of anyone's imagination yet), and I would press PLAY on my favorite song and start to imagine. I would imagine myself in the Maccabi Haifa lineup, executing great plays — really feeling it. The higher level in imagery is when you can smell the grass, hear the spectators and feel your touch on the ball. The more you can activate all your senses in your imagination, the more your body will believe that it's possible and will not be surprised when you need to do these things during the game in real-time.

Imagery is one of the tools that made me believe that I could make it to the seniors. My imagination took me out of that terrible bus and made me feel good even though I actually had every reason not to.

As such, from this day on you are going to imagine your own success at least once a day.

How can you do this? There are no rules.

On your way to practice you can listen to whichever song sends you flying, and imagine yourself doing well. On the night before practice or a game, close your eyes for a few minutes and imagine the yourself on the field. Imagine yourself succeeding, playing exactly the way you want to. The following day, give yourself ten minutes before practice or the game begins. Find a corner in the locker room, close your eyes for 60 seconds and imagine, simply getting your brain accustomed to seeing you succeed…When that happens you won't have any choice but to move and to aspire to be that player.

I suggest that you imagine two good actions, one offensive and one defensive. If you play offense, then one good offensive play could be, for example, to assist on a goal and one defensive play could be to steal the ball. If you play defense then a good offensive play could be to clear the ball by launching a quick attack and a good defensive play could be to steal the ball in a 1 v 1. Simply see it happening.

Stage Three of Confidence: Focus on Yourself and Do Not Compare Yourself with Others

Between you and me, there will always be someone who is just that much more agile than you are, just as there will always be someone much slower and weaker than you are.

But that's the problem with comparisons. When we compare ourselves to others we always come out worse and our self-confidence drops. Why? Because our brain is always happier looking for (and finding) what we lack and what we don't do well enough. The worst thing about comparisons is that they make us judge and criticize ourselves, which…as you must know by now… is what makes you lose your self-confidence.

The main point then that you need to understand here is that the only person that you need to compare yourself with is the person you were the day before. In other words, your aim is to look at yourself each day and to make sure that you've improved a little since the day before, which means, making sure that today will be better than yesterday, and that tomorrow will be even better.

Focusing on yourself means staying an extra 10 to 15 minutes after everyone else has left after practice to improve another element of your game. Moreover, focusing on yourself is not hoping that your competition for a position will demonstrate less ability so that you can take their place in the lineup. It means improving your own professional abilities so that you can be the best in the country (or the world) in your position. Your aim from this day on is to become the best player you can be. **Others are of no interest to you because you have no control over them.** It is important to learn how to live with the fact that you cannot control other people, and focusing on others can only lower your confidence. Remember the example I gave you of myself when I was playing for Maccabi Haifa? What do you think would have happened if I'd compared myself to Alon Harazi or Avishai Zano? I wouldn't have had a chance.

Focus on yourself and do not compare yourself to anyone else. Whenever you find yourself thinking things along the line of "If only I was as fast as they are," or "I don't have their height or build," then that is the time to silence the voice you are hearing and to say to yourself, "I am proud of what I have, these are my abilities, and I am going to win with them."

Stage Four of Confidence: Focus on the Steps towards Your Goal —Not on Your Goal Itself!

We are now going to start moving from internal confidence to external confidence, and as such the fourth stage of self-confidence is: focus on the steps you need to take to reach your goal, not on the goal itself!

Imagine an attacking midfielder who plans on scoring a hat-trick in tomorrow's game. All that midfielder is thinking about is, "I have to score a hat-trick"…"I have to score a hat-trick"…"I have to score a hat-trick."

My question to you is whether that midfielder can score a hat-trick when all they are thinking about is their desire to score.

If you focus on scoring, it simply isn't going to happen. On the other hand, if you focus on the steps you need to take to be in a position to score, the odds of scoring a hat-trick shoot up. In other words, most players make the mistake in games of focusing on their goal and forget to do those things (the path) that will lead them to there. Then what happens is that their minds are occupied with the future and with what they want to achieve. Their heads are so stuck in the future they forget to play in the present. In the end they reach the end of the game without doing almost anything and without performing to their true potential. All this happens not because they do not have the ability but because their minds are focused on their final goal instead of on the steps they need to take to reach it.

191

In other words, if you focus on professional success, you are not going to do well. On the other hand, if you focus on the steps to success, then the odds of your dream becoming a reality improve.

One of the stories I share when I give workshops or lectures, a story that helps my own players to understand the importance of "focusing on steps, not on your goal" goes like this:

I'll admit, this story may seem misplaced, but stick with me because if you understand it you'll learn the most important rule for self-confidence.

Sometimes when I give lectures I share a story about two friends, Terry and Andy, who are stuck on opposite sides of a river. Terry is safe from danger on one side of the river, while Andy is stuck with a broken leg on the other. Terry has 90 minutes to save Andy from a fire that is spreading, but there is another problem — there is a rough wild river with piranhas, sharks, dragons — you name it — that will kill anyone who tries to cross it.

OK, now imagine the river, with Terry standing on one bank, the terrified Andy standing on the other, and a river of fire and teeth between them!

Then, I ask someone from the audience, "Tell me, what is Terry's goal?"

The answer I get from everyone is, "Terry's goal is to save Andy."

OK, and then I ask again, "And tell me, if Terry focuses on needing to save Andy as the goal, and simply goes for it, what will happen?"

And then everyone answers, "Well, obviously by rushing to save Andy, Terry will get eaten alive or burned to a crisp by a dragon and die."

Then, I ask them again, "So you tell me — what do you think Terry should do instead of focusing on the goal and running for it?"

The players then start to understand that Terry can only save Andy by focusing only on the steps that will lead to Andy.

Terry could build a bridge over the river, hire a hot-air balloon or ask Renaldo over to deal with the sharks. But what is more important in this story is that in order to save Andy, Terry needs to focus on the steps and actions that need to be taken instead of blindly rushing over to the other side of the river.

Just like Terry needs to focus on the steps needed to take to save Andy, so you too need to focus firstly on the steps that will help you achieve your goal in the game.

In other words, if you're a main striker or a midfielder who wants to score a brace in a game, then stop focusing on scoring those two goals and start focusing on the professional acts that will lead you to put the ball in the net twice, such as:

1. Closing down on the defenders for 90 minutes.
2. Running to the short corner of the 18 yard box, no matter what.
3. Maintaining eye contact with the midfielder who is knows your plays well (which, by the way, is exactly what Trezeguet did).

Or on the other hand, if you're a defender, goalkeeper, defender or fullback who wants to finish the game with a clean sheet, then stop telling yourself, "I mustn't allow them to score today," and instead, ask yourself, "What are the three professional acts I need to focus on to increase my odds of keeping the a clean sheet?"

The answer that will come to mind could be things like:

1. Play close to your defender and don't allow the ball to get between you.
2. Stick to your main striker at all times.
3. Commit to playing simple defense.
4. Communicate with all four defense players.

Can you see the difference?

I realize that your main goal is to succeed in the future, but successful footballers think of the future for only a short time. They pinpoint their goal, and as soon as they've done so, they immediately return their focus to the professional steps and acts that will lead them to that goal.

So from this day on, stop focusing on the result you want to achieve in any upcoming game and start to focus on the steps that will get you there.

To sum up, the fourth stage of building confidence is: Before each game, focus on three professional acts that you have control over, acts that will bring you closer to and improve the odds of attaining your goal in the game. You can call them mini-goals. Only mini-goals will help you to achieve your main goal.

Stage Five of Confidence: Show Confidence Long before the Game Starts

After you've built up your internal confidence we want you to let it out so that it can become external confidence and peak ability, and that is the easy part. This is the part when you you're your confidence physically, by using body language. This is where we stop talking and thinking about confidence and start showing it.

If the fourth stage of confidence was to focus on the steps we need to take to succeed and not on success itself, then the fifth stage says: Show your confidence long before the game or practice starts.

By this I mean that your aim is, from the moment you enter the locker room, to shower everyone with positive energy: players, masseurs, doctors, staff members. Why do we want to do that? Because when we show confidence, smile, talk to everyone (instead of staring at the floor) what we're actually doing is getting our energy, blood and adrenalin flowing through our bodies. That puts us in the zone and makes us feel confident in ourselves; and that feeling of confidence simply gets pulled into the game.

One small note regarding this stage — I do not mean that you need to act like cheerleaders before practice or a game…not at all.

What I do want is for your presence to be noticed as soon as you enter the locker room.

That is what I used to do before games — and by the way — it is what I still do when I give lectures or workshops. Instead of going off to be on my own, I jump around and shout, put loud music on in the hall, I talk to people and I laugh with them.

Before the last workshop I gave, to 100 hungry footballers, I could feel the tension start to build up in me, and because I know myself well I asked my staff to welcome the guests and told them I would be right back. I got into the elevator, went down to the parking lot, started my car and put my favorite song on at full volume — Kelly Clarkson's *Stronger (What Doesn't Kill You)*. As always, that song had me going wild, gave me an adrenalin rush and sent my energy levels sky-high. I could feel confidence flood my body, and when I knew that I was flooded with energy, I left the car and ran back to the hall.

It was eight forty-five; only five minutes before the conference was due to begin.

Boom!

I felt like fire...I spoke for a few minutes more with everyone and at nine o'clock I started the workshop feeling highly confident.

By the way, I didn't invent this; this is exactly what European footballers, famous lecturers and artists do before their important events. If it works for them I have no doubt that it'll work for you whenever you use it.

Your confidence, just like your body, needs a warm-up before a game! When you're in the locker room with your teammates an hour before the game is a perfect time to send your confidence through the roof.

Show confidence long before the game or training session starts

Stage Six of Confidence: Show Confidence with Your Body Language

In other words: From the instant you hit the grass to warm up, you need to run, move, breath, keep your body straight and proud, displaying the same amount of confidence as you would if you'd already won the game, as if you're hungry for another game to crush your opponent in, even though the game hasn't even started yet.

But why do we need to use body language that shows confidence?

Your body language shapes you, determines how you feel about yourself and how others feel about you, before you even begin to do anything.

Studies have shown that by doing certain movements that show confidence — even if you aren't really feeling self-confident — can have an impact on your chances of succeeding in doing things that you would never be able to do with body language that shouts out weakness.

It seems that something happens in our brains when we stand in a way that shows confidence. What happens is that doing high-power poses affects the testosterone and cortisol levels in our brains.

Don't worry. You don't need to know what all that means, but what you do need to know is that hormones are secreted in your body when you use power poses and body language that raise your confidence. When we use the body language of confidence, testosterone levels increase in both women and men, giving them more confidence and making them more aggressive and competitive, whereas cortisol (the stress hormone that kicks in when we're afraid) drops. This happens when your posture is firm and steady. And guess what you need to beat your opponent? Exactly! Aggressiveness and competitiveness.

We do not want to wait until our confidence goes up on its own or until we make a good pass before it goes up. We want to boost it before the game even starts. As such, your body language is an excellent tool to use to raise your confidence before the game. This means that from this day on, you are going to go onto the field like a gladiator. You are going to:

1. Hold your head up high.
2. Look straight into the eyes of your opponent.

3. Breathe deeply.
4. Pull your shoulders back,
5. Give a cunning smile to show that you're going to win the game.

Choose one movement to add, and take it with you onto the field.

Stage Seven of Confidence: Show Confidence after Mistakes!

If you implement all the principles and steps you've received here…if you accept yourself, imagine winning before games, stop comparing yourself with anyone else, show your confidence in your body language — but then ask for permission to leave the field after a mistake, you will do yourself and your confidence more damage than if you were to shoot yourself in the foot.

Why?

Because if you cannot recover quickly from mistakes when playing, your body language will tell everyone that you don't truly want to succeed. Then, the next time you lose the ball or don't execute well, you will get used to giving in — and that is not what we want happening. It is not the type of player you want to be.

I can tell you right now that not every game you play will be perfect, but what is no-less important is that you don't create a name for yourself as weak and a pushover, as easily offended, or as someone who avoids playing.

This stage is super-critical, and as such your aim from this day on is to train yourself to recover quickly from crises. In other words, from this day on I want you to internalize the magic word for a quick recovery and that word is NEXT!

This magic word (surprisingly) says the following:

Just as you will have good plays during the game, so you will also make mistakes. The mistakes are irrelevant. What is important is the way in which you respond to them.

The best footballers in the world are not those who never have to overcome obstacles or crises.

The players who have achieved it all are the ones who learned how to control their reactions to what was happening on field.

You will not be able to control everything that happens to you in your next game (we have no control over the referee, the weather, the spectators). We do, however, have 100% control over how we respond to anything that happens to us during the game.

In April 2008, the U.S. Women's national team played against Costa Rica to qualify for the 2008 Beijing Olympics. They won 3-0 and qualified.

The match was played in a massive dust storm with high winds. When the first half finished, the US team had not yet managed to score.

What did the players have to say about the game?

Well, Heather O'Reilly said that although they were surprised at halftime, they remained composed and very positive. Nobody freaked out, and they continued to believe in themselves and in their preparation.

Amy Rodriquez said how great it was to play games in different weather conditions. She had never played in a sand storm before, and she enjoyed the opportunity, saying that you don't always get to play on a perfect field in perfect weather.

And what did Natasha Kai have to say? That you need to be ready to play under any circumstances – that's a part of being a professional.

Your response to every move in the game is your weapon for success, because a player who gets stuck and who drops their head after every mistake is allowing the mistake to control them. On the other hand, when you respond to the mistake by moving on to your next move and maintaining your belief despite the last mistake, you are the one controlling the mistake and your own self-confidence.

Successful players respond to events.

The others freeze and get stuck in the past.

That is why your key word for the next game is: NEXT

This means that when a move is over (whether it worked or not doesn't matter) — you say to yourself, NEXT... time for the next move.

You've given the ball away in opponent territory? Say NEXT to the next move.

You've scored a goal? Tell yourself NEXT and go in search of the next goal.

The game started badly? Say NEXT to the next move.

Successful players understand that you cannot turn the clock back, and as such, overanalyzing mistakes only distracts them from the game, so they make sure to move from one move to the next as fast as they possibly can, and they do this is by repeating the word NEXT in their minds.

It's OK to feel a little disappointed if you didn't execute a play as you expected it to but the truth is (don't tell anyone) not everyone has to know that you're disappointed. People can smell when others lack confidence and are afraid, so in games you want to show that "business is as usual" and that everything is just fine, even if inside you are disappointed or angry.

I'm sure that at some time in your career you've seen **players who are afraid or who lack confidence.**

What do their shoulders do? **They droop.**

Where are they looking? **Half down, half at the game.**

How do they run? **Hesitantly.**

How do they react after a mistake? **With disappointment, and they return to their positions slowly, mumbling "what a drag" to themselves.**

What do you think of that player now? Not much, right?

Would you want people to see you in the same way? I know that you wouldn't!

So don't give anyone the opportunity to smell fear or lack in confidence on you.

Imagine for just a moment that you've lost an important ball, or that you've made a mistake. At that precise moment, you want to regain your balance fast, within three seconds or less. What this means, is that you are looking up, your head is held high, you're keeping your eye on the ball — and most importantly, you are immediately on the lookout for the next move... NEXT...this means returning to the defense, running to close down on your opponent, encouraging yourself before your next play.

Stage Eight of Confidence: Play like the Kid That You Were the First Time You Saw a Ball

Children are fearless, and they have no obstacles in their heads. They are not afraid of failure. They love taking risks — and they always get what they want.

Think about it. After all, children are fearless and when they want something they stop at nothing to get it. When a baby is learning how to walk they fall down hundreds of times, and then what do they do? They get up within seconds, smile, and move towards their goal.

What does this have to do with football?

Sometimes we reach a point where this game, that we like so much, suddenly becomes a career and profession, and we find ourselves with commitments, goals, responsibility, and expectations. We become afraid of failure, and develop a need to prove ourselves.

Commitment and the drive to succeed enter the picture of this game that we loved so much as children. It's not that that is a bad thing, but without even noticing, something really important and critical to our success has disappeared from our lives, and that thing is enjoyment of the game. Between you and me, we both know that as soon as a player brings enjoyment into the game, all those obstacles I mentioned disappear within a second! They disappear entirely!

Why?

Because where there is enjoyment there is no fear and there are no limits.

Where there is enjoyment there is also creativity and freedom.

When you're having fun time flies by. You're focused, you're paying attention, you can control the ball easily and you can stop the ball with your heel with no problem at all.

Why? Because that is what we do when we're having fun.

So what I've done here is added a list of 12 characteristics of children (and you can swap the word "children" with the world "winner" because children are true winners). Please go through this list and choose one or more characteristics that you want to have again (or that you want to add) to the way you play the game...

Twelve characteristics that children have:

1. Determination
2. Fearlessness of making mistakes
3. Pleasure from taking risks
4. An ability to dream big
5. Do not care what anyone thinks of them
6. Daring
7. Courage
8. Are able to do what they think they should do — and not what everyone wants them to do
9. After making a mistake, they can get up and carry on as if nothing has happened
10. They love trying out new things

11. They give themselves compliments — they do not wait for feedback from others

12. They are not afraid to look silly

These are all characteristics that you'll want to add to the way you play the game, now and in the future.

As such I want you to try to remember the first time you played football; a time when you didn't feel pressure but excitement and positive expectation that something good was about to happen. The more you remind yourself that the reason you play football is because you chose to and not because anyone made you, the more you will feel relaxed and focused — and that is when you will start to recognize the opportunities on the field that you didn't notice before.

Have fun and take your inner child with you onto the field at the start of each game, not only the serious player in you.

Now you have eight stages that are cast in stone:

1. Accept yourself just the way you are! What you have in you now is excellent and it will help you to win.

2. Imagine yourself succeeding at least once a day.

3. Focus on yourself and do not compare yourself with others

4. Focus on the step to success, and not on the success itself.

5. Show confidence already in the locker room, long before the game or practice starts.

6. Show confidence with your body language, from the first minute of the game.

7. Show confidence after mistakes (NEXT)!

8. Become a child again. Being a footballer is your own choice, enjoy this choice.

Three-Minute Mental Preparation for the Game

In addition to those fixed rules, I want to give you a simple way to prepare yourself mentally before a game, so that you can start every game highly confident. What we are going to do together is I'm going to show you how to think the night before a game, and how you can instruct your brain to be clear and relaxed on the day of the game (and stop it from bothering you with thoughts on the most important day of the week).

What is important is to follow my instructions, so that in the future you will be able to do this on your own. I recommend you use this method over the coming week, before every practice and every game.

Before we begin I should tell you that the easiest way to damage your self-confidence is to set your expectations too high before a game. In other words, this is a big mistake and it could lower your self-confidence. A footballer with too high expectations of themselves is usually one whose self-confidence can be expected to plummet.

You probably want to ask me now, "Hold on, Eitan, why would it be a mistake to expect the best of myself? After all, high expectations are what help me to improve and to be a better player, aren't they?"

Well, actually they aren't!

The real problem with having too high expectations of yourself before a game…like when you tell yourself for example, "I must score a hat-trick today," or "I mustn't lose any balls today,"…is that what you're really doing is expecting yourself to be perfect. Then, when you can't fulfill your own expectations and you make a mistake in the game or lose the ball, your self-confidence plummets because you didn't stand up to your own expectations.

Generally speaking, players who set their expectations too high usually find it hard to get over mistakes and to move on.

Don't get me wrong...I want you to set yourself big career goals, and I also want you to aspire to scoring twice every game, or to keeping a clean sheet (if you're a goalkeeper or a defender), and I do want you to dream big! But...I don't want you to demand perfection of yourself, because to aspire to perfection before a game only puts more pressure on you and makes you play it safe, and when you play it safe you're really playing to "not make mistakes." A footballer who plays with the aim of "not making mistakes," really does not make mistakes, but also never gets ahead professionally because their fear limits their thinking and prevents them from taking risks. What they then find themselves doing is avoiding the game and losing their head and their self- confidence after every mistake.

That is not what we want to happen.

Many players confuse expectations with goals and the difference needs to be clear: High expectations put you under unnecessary pressure and make you feel obliged. Goals, on the other hand, get you excited in a positive way, get your adrenaline going and make you want to do what you need to.

You have high expectations when you tell yourself things like, "I have to"..."I mustn't"..."it's all or nothing."

You have goals when you tell yourself that "I want to do that"…"I'm ready to do that"…"I don't want to do that."

So the way to raise your confidence includes two stages:

Stage One: Getting rid of all your expectations.

Stage Two: Incorporating "mini-goals" in your game.

What does this mean?

That's very simple.

Stage One: Get Rid of Expectations — Throw out Your High Expectations of Yourself
Statements such as "I have to be perfect today," "I mustn't lose a single ball today," "I'm going to have the game of a lifetime today," or "This is my last chance to win," are all statements that crush your self-confidence because they require you to be perfect — and the only thing that the need to be perfect does is put you under pressure. As such, your first step before any game is to recognize these expectations and then discard them so that you can stop focusing on them and start focusing on actions that you can control.

Stage Two: Mini-Goals— Focus Only on Professional Actions That You Control

Before a game, choose to focus on three professional acts that are in your control. In other words, ask yourself what you can do on the field today that will work every time.

For example, "To close in on the main striker," "To protect my position," "Not to get stuck on mistakes but to just carry on no matter what," "To kick decisively to the goal without apologizing or caring what anyone thinks," "To go 1 v 1 and to feel fine when it doesn't go perfectly every time," "To communicate with my defenders," or "To direct the player next to me."

In other words, what we are going to do is to use Stage Four, which says "Don't focus on success but on the steps to success." Don't focus on scoring but on the steps that will help you to score, don't think about your opponent scoring against you but on the steps that will help you keep a clean sheet.

The easiest way, therefore, to prepare yourself mentally before a game, is to sit at home the day before game day and to identify and discard all those too high expectations you have of yourself. You need to replace them with the goals that are in your control, and to make them a part of your game.

How do we actually do this?

Let's do it together.

Say that today is the day before a game.

Now I want you to find a quiet place or corner for yourself, at home or wherever you are right now — a place where nobody will interrupt you for the next few minutes. You can sit upright, lie down, whatever is more comfortable for you, and when you're ready and relaxed, what I want you to do is take a deep breath through your nose, hold it for two seconds and slowly let the air out through your mouth.

Again, take a deep breath through your nose, hold it for a couple of seconds and let it out slowly through your mouth (notice how your stomach rises as you breathe in).

Take a third breath, hold it for two seconds, and let it out through your mouth.

I want you to carry on breathing like that while we build up the self-confidence before the game that will help you to win.

While you're breathing, I want you to take a moment to think about what too high expectations you may have of yourself now, and think about those things that you usually tell yourself before a game, such as, "I must not make any mistakes," "This is a crucial game for me," "I must prove to everyone that I deserve this," "This game has to be all or nothing," "This is my only and last chance"...whatever comes to mind...and what I want you to do now is to take your expectations, imagine these statements, and start throwing all of them into your imaginary trashcan. Simply take each sentence and throw it out.

Do you feel like you have to be perfect and that you must never make any mistakes? Then tell yourself, "I don't owe anyone anything. I am playing for myself."

You are allowed to make mistakes, and it is OK to make mistakes. You're human.

Do you think that you have to prove how good you are to everyone? Drop it. You don't have to prove anything to anyone! Throw that thought out because it is not helping you. You need to play for yourself, this is your profession and you chose it. You do not owe anything to anyone.

You may already be able to feel a sense of relief spreading through you simply from deciding for yourself to play without expectations and to create mini-goals that are in your control instead.

OK, take a few more moments to rid yourself of expectations and you should feel a lot lighter and relaxed now.

After you've rid yourself of your too high expectations, those that were putting you under pressure, it is time to choose your mini-goals that will boost your self-confidence.

What I want you to do while you're breathing is to think of two things (only two) that you are in control of and that you can perform in the game; two professional moves that you can do well every time, without any problems.

These moves need to be the simplest there are, and they will help you achieve your objective in the game.

If you play offense and your aim in the game is to score or to assist then imagine executing those moves that are in your control — it can be running to the short corner for every attack, closing down the defender, asking for the ball… and imagine yourself doing it.

If you play defense, and it is important to you to keep a clean sheet, then you're going to choose to mark your opponent closely, to defend your side well, to maintain eye contact and to communicate with the player next to you. See it happening and feel the confidence flow through your body because you know that you will definitely be able to do this in the game.

Take a deep breath of confidence. Feel the air enter your body and spread, filling all your muscles with confidence.

Let it out. Excellent.

Take another breath of confidence, feel your stomach expand as you inhale, hold it in your stomach for a couple of seconds and let it out very slowly.

Excellent, and when you can feel your confidence right down in your feet (and when you know that your confidence depends only on you) I want you to take one last deep breath of confidence, and to slowly smile like a winner.

Welcome! You're now ready to conquer the field.

Now is the time to get to your game or practice with your secret weapon, and remember, you already have the confidence you need to succeed!

You are already doing well and you do not need to prove anything to anyone, so good luck, go out there and play for yourself today.

Enjoy the game — today you have become a fearless player!

Chapter 12

The Winner's Self-Talk – to Read to Yourself before Every Game

If you've reached this point in the book, you can be proud of yourself. You have come very far. You may not have noticed, but your body has already internalized earlier chapters. You'll be surprised to discover that already at your next game you'll be able to play with more confidence, take new risks, and calmly execute those last actions, ending the game with a smile and with the enjoyment and results that will get you another step closer to your dream.

By now you know me well, and as you know I always like to give a little bit more. As such, I want to give you another gift in this chapter, and this time I'm going to do the work for you, making it easier for you to internalize the thoughts that fearless footballers have, so that you'll be able to take risks with confidence, succeed in them, and develop your competitive edge over your opponents.

After all, in the end the fastest way to improve what you get from your career is by looking at what you give of yourself to your career.

The first question you need to ask yourself is, "What thoughts am I walking around with today?"

Your body is a tool used by your mind and it works only in the way your mind trains it to work.

For example, a player whose head droops after losing a ball is a player whose mind has taught them to be great at taking things badly. In contrast, a player who moves on after a mistake and wins the game is a player whose mind has trained them to take responsibility and to play like a leader in all circumstances.

I have therefore prepared a personal letter based on the personal thoughts of the best players in the world. These are thoughts that I've been collecting for years. Some I wrote from my own experience as a footballer, and others I developed from observation, research, and my own personal work with hundreds of players in Israel and around the world.

My aim in writing this letter was to create the perfect line of thought that courageous and fearless footballers use.

I now want that line of thought to become a part of you — so that you too can attain your dream and eradicate the obstacles that may hold you back on your way there.

Now, when you read this letter, I want you to read it to yourself and to feel as if you wrote it yourself.

This letter may seem new to you at first, but after reading it a few times, it will become an inseparable part of your personality and character, and it will be impossible for you to not become a better player that the one you are today.

So when you read it now, you can read it silently or aloud, but mean the words you are reading because the more you mean them, the stronger your belief will become. If you truly want to start every game raring to go, I suggest you read it with your earphones on while you listen to your favorite song.

Take a deep assuring breath…and we'll get going:

I am so proud to be _____ (say your name), a footballer with aspirations and dreams!

I realize that I am still in the process of attaining my goals and my dream of a career _____ I am not trying to impress others, or trying to be like any other person to satisfy other people!

I did not come into this world to satisfy anyone else, and today, when I go onto the field, the only recognition I need to receive is my own.

Today, when I go onto the field, I will relate to myself as a successful senior player from the very first minute, because I know that I have all the qualities needed to lead this team to victory.

Today will be the day I take risks that can help me in my game, because I know that behind every risk there is the opportunity for success. I prefer to take a risk in opponent territory than to regret not taking action and asking myself later when I get home what would have happened if I had.

I accept that not everyone will like it, but I now know not to take anything personally, because I know that every person has their own world view and that it is fine if people have different desires from my own _____ they too are human beings. I understand that a footballer who is afraid of taking risks is one who demonstrates boring ability _____ and who has no place being on the field with the best players. As such, when I go onto the field today I am going to play for myself and for the child in me that has overcome every obstacle in my way to make it to where I am today.

At the end of the day when I look at myself in the mirror, I need to know that I have given all that I have to give, that I have used my courage to the fullest, and that I have dared to make the moves that I planned and ran through in my mind.

Today I say goodbye to that young child I used to be who waited for admiration, and I welcome the improved player that I am _____ a player with self-respect.

Today I choose to not assume, and to not search for recognition or feedback from others, because I know that these things are not up to me _____ and because I get my strength to do well from myself, not from others.

I know that those people who once occupied my thoughts and whose approval I would wait for are not really thinking about me right now, because they are concerned with themselves and with their own lives. As such if they do not invest any of their thoughts or energy in me there is no reason for me to waste the strength and energy I need to succeed on them.

I will not give up until I succeed.

My nature has always told me not to give up.

I have always followed my dream all the way to the end.

I have always done extra practice whenever I could and that is what has made me the unique player I am today.

My character is a gift from above.

When I run onto the field today I will not pay anyone any attention. Today I fully appreciate myself. I know that I perform best and more easily when I am my own best friend! I was born loved and respected by my parents. I am an honest, sincere person with an enormous heart, and I care about my close ones. This makes me a special person before I even step onto the field!

I am proud of who I am!

I like myself and my qualities!

It is OK for things not to go right because that's the nature of the game, but I know that today I have come here to do the things I am capable of.

Today I have taken this game on myself.

I have used my daring.

I have gone for the ball.

I have been involved.

I have made real movements to receive the ball.

I have created plays.

I have received the ball in the half and looked for ways to get behind a player.

Whenever I think about losing the ball I will go hard for the ball because that is what gets me into the game, and I want to thank my fear for giving me a sign and helping me to become more involved in the game again.

Today, and every day I am alive, I choose to accept and respect myself unconditionally, as a person before a footballer. I know that the fastest way to feel good on the field is to first feel good at home with who I am as a person, so from now on, already in the upcoming practice and game, I choose to play for myself and for the child within me who grabs with both hands every opportunity to play the best game of their life.

I promise to accept myself, unrelated to my professional success or to what people think or expect of me. I know that my results in football cannot have any impact on my personality as a person, because the only person who gives me confirmation that I am good is me _____ and I know that the only true recognition I need in life is the recognition I award myself.

I am already a successful player with a past filled with successes, achievements and vast experience as a footballer.

Now, with all this courage flowing constantly through my body getting stronger, I cannot wait even one second longer before I hit the field and show everyone what I am capable of.

I now know that everything I have sacrificed in life was worth it, everything I have dreamed of was worth it _____ and I want more.

Today I will persist until I succeed.

I forgive everyone and everyone forgives me.

Everything I do at practice and with my friends from down the road I can do easily in games.

I love myself.

I am proud of my aspirations.

Today my dream will be expressed at the game.

I am a fearless footballer and I know it!

Amen

Bonus Chapter

The 10 Iron Rules for Living with Everlasting Confidence

I wrote this chapter on May 7, 2014, a few hours after winning the Israel State Cup Final for the second time in my career — this time as the mental coach of the Hapoel Ironi Kiryat Shmona F.C.

The first time I held up the State Cup trophy was on May 27, 2003, 11 years earlier when I was playing for Hapoel Ramat Gan F.C. (I was 19 years old at the time).

Those 11 years meant nothing to my body because the body remembers everything! That same crazy feeling of release, satisfaction, joy, and happiness for achieving my goals, swept through my body like wildfire.

The time was 3:34 a.m.

I tried to fall asleep, but I simply couldn't — my body was still being flooded with adrenaline.

So I simply began to write.

I wrote and wrote and wrote, until even the "notes" on my iPhone were fed up with me.

And eventually I fell asleep.

When I woke up I looked at my phone and discovered I had written down all the points, insights and principles for success that had guided me and the players I have worked with as a mental consultant for achievement.

I have condensed all those points into just ten iron principles that have guided me from my first State Cup a decade before as a player, to a second State Cup as a mental consultant. And now I want you to have them too.

I have called these ten principles "The Ten Iron Rules."

And here they are…

The Ten Iron Rules

1. **Never give up your dream** — it is not that hard to fulfill. You are simply making more of it than it is.

2. **Do not listen to yourself too much** — you are not always right when you think that you are incapable!

3. **Be extreme, ambitious, delusional** — logical people get nowhere in life.

4. **Fall in love with uncertainty** — that is where your biggest opportunities for breakthroughs in life lie. Your greatest chance at success lies within that thing you are most afraid of.

5. **Always focus on what you want to achieve and not on what you are afraid could go wrong** — yes, if you focus on success you may not always succeed, but if you focus on failure you are sure to crash.

6. **Your quality of life depends on your ability to give and not on your desire to receive** — helping someone else do well is always more moving than helping yourself to do well.

7. **Wanting to be perfect is the lowest standard of the science of success** — perfectionists will always find something wrong with themselves to make themselves feel they are not good enough. Don't go there; instead choose to make as many mistakes as you can because failure is the most important stage on the way to winning.

8. **Football does not build character, football exposes character** — your character will be built up quietly, when nobody is watching you.

9. Find someone (today) who believes in you more than you believe in yourself — you are going to need that person more than you think.

10. **Always try to be around people who are better than you, they will make you better without any effort** — as the old saying goes...if you lie down with dogs you get up with fleas. If you hang out with eagles you'll have no choice but to fly.

New Beginning

We have reached the end of the book, but in truth the book isn't done — you're only at the start.

I would like you to think of this book as your own personal mental coach. You can pick it up any time you feel you need reinforcement, support, or to hear the right words before a game.

One of my players once told me, "Eitan, this book goes into my duffle bag before my shoes, my shin guards, and my deodorant." I really hope that that's the way it'll be for you too.

How to Use This Book during the Season to Keep Your Confidence and Ability Up

My advice to you is — choose a page (never mind which) and read a few lines before you go to sleep the night before a game — that is the best time to direct your thoughts towards winning (you can, of course, read this book in your free time during the week, I even recommend it).

I have one more thing to say to you — and that is Thank You.

You are the reason that I do what I do.

The fact that you have invested your time and energy in receiving the knowledge here says a lot about you, and I can't wait to see you emerge and play with nothing holding you back— because that is what you are destined for in this world!

You are the Fearless Footballer.

Bless you,

Eitan

Meet Eitan Azaria

When it comes to the world of psychology and mental training, Eitan Azaria is considered very young; only 32. His 15 years of experience as a player in the Israeli premier league and the Israeli national team are rare on a very unique level. Only a few 32-year-old footballers can look back at their career filled with so much success: 2 championships with Maccabi Haifa, 2 cups (the State Cup and the Toto Cup), and over 60 appearances with various Israeli national teams. He was promoted league to the premier league after taking first place (with Maccabi Herzliya).

He has over 10,000 subscribers and over 1,000 satisfied footballers who have fulfilled their potential using the mental processes he suited to their personal needs. Winning the State Cup with Hapoel Ironi Kiryat Shmona F.C. (a young team with a limited budget) as their mental consultant can probably not be put down to pure luck.

Eitan is onto something.

Without being too complimentary, there must be something about going onto the field and trying something new during every practice for 20 years that enabled Eitan to make more mistakes than anyone, therefore understanding what works and what doesn't, and as a result – to share his roadmap to success with others.

Through everything Eitan does today, from the moment he gets up in the morning, he helps people realize the tremendous potential they have inside, and so they can become role models and a source of inspiration for bringing change to the world.

The tools and methods that Eitan discovered, tried and tested have proven themselves time and time again on every field he has played on as a footballer and through every player he has mentally coached.

Eitan believes that:

Every person can realize the potential they have inside.

In each and every person there is greater innate potential than they believe exists.

The only barrier separating us from fulfilling the full potential we have is ourselves. We stop ourselves from being more successful. And the key to fulfilling our full potential lies in improving our connection with ourselves – because when potential is realized, dreams come true.

Are you ready to jump to your next level?

Contact Eitan today

By email: eitan@eitanazaria.com

Made in the USA
Middletown, DE
06 June 2016